W9-AUY-001

George Washington Carver

SCIENTIST AND EDUCATOR

Black Americans of Achievement

LEGACY EDITION

Muhammad Ali

Maya Angelou

Josephine Baker

George Washington Carver

Johnnie Cochran

Frederick Douglass

W.E.B. Du Bois

Marcus Garvey

Savion Glover

Alex Haley

Jimi Hendrix

Gregory Hines

Langston Hughes

Jesse Jackson

Scott Joplin

Coretta Scott King

Martin Luther King, Jr.

Malcolm X

Bob Marley

Thurgood Marshall

Barack Obama

Jesse Owens

Rosa Parks

Colin Powell

Condoleezza Rice

Chris Rock

Sojourner Truth

Harriet Tubman

Nat Turner

Booker T. Washington

Oprah Winfrey

Tiger Woods

Black Americans of Achievement
LEGACY EDITION

George Washington Carver

SCIENTIST AND EDUCATOR

Dennis Abrams

CHELSEA HOUSE
PUBLISHERS
An imprint of Infobase Publishing

George Washington Carver

Copyright © 2008 by Infobase Publishing

Chelsea House
An imprint of Infobase Publishing
132 West 31st Street
New York NY 10001

Library of Congress Cataloging-in-Publication Data

Abrams, Dennis, 1960-
  George Washington Carver : scientist and educator / Dennis Abrams.
    p. cm. -- (Black Americans of achievement legacy edition)
  Includes bibliographical references and index.
  ISBN 978-0-7910-9717-5 (hardcover)
  1. Carver, George Washington, 1864?-1943--Juvenile literature. 2. African American agriculturists--Biography--Juvenile literature. 3. Agriculturists--United States--Biography-- Juvenile literature. I. Title. II. Series.

  S417.C3A54 2008
  630.92--dc22
  [B]   2007035677

Series design by Keith Trego
Cover design by Keith Trego and Jooyoung An

Printed in the United States of America

Bang ML 10 9 8 7 6 5 4 3 2 1

This book is printed on acid-free paper.

All links and web addresses were checked and verified to be correct at the time of publication. Because of the dynamic nature of the web, some addresses and links may have changed since publication and may no longer be valid.

Contents

The Man, the Myth

In October 1932, *American Magazine*, a popular periodical of the time, published an article by James Saxon Childers entitled "A Boy Who Was Traded for a Horse." The article, which was later published in a condensed version in *Reader's Digest* in February 1937, brought fame to the man who for years had worked in near obscurity: George Washington Carver.

In the article, Childers gave Carver complete credit for increasing peanut production in the South after an invasion of boll weevils had nearly destroyed the region's cotton crops. The article claimed that Carver had made nearly 300 "useful products" from peanuts and another 100 from sweet potatoes and that experts said that "he has done more than any other living man to rehabilitate agriculture in the South."

More than that, the article described a man whom white Americans, even those who were prejudiced against African Americans, could feel comfortable respecting. The author drew a picture of a kindly, harmless, hardworking gentleman who worked in the "humble" field of agriculture—a man who gave credit to divine inspiration for his accomplishments:

A stooped old Negro, carrying an armful of wild flowers shuffled along through the dust of an Alabama road toward one of the buildings of Tuskegee Institute. His thin body bent by the years, his hair white beneath a ragged cap, he seemed pathetically lost on the campus of an educational institution. Poor old fellow; I had seen hundreds like him. Totally ignorant, unable to read and write, they shamble along Southern roads in search of odd jobs.

At the door of one of the buildings, I saw a trim little secretary hurry up to the bent old Negro: "That delegation from Washington is waiting for you, Doctor Carver."

Fantastic as it seemed, this shabbily-clad old man was none other than the distinguished Negro scientist of Tuskegee Institute, Dr. George Washington Carver, renowned for his chemical wizardry.

Born a slave child, he began life without even a name. He never knew his father or mother. To this day he doesn't know when he was born, though he figures his age at over 70. All his life he has been joyously at work with every-day things, making something out of nothing, or next to nothing.

No one can adequately report the strange feeling of spiritual betterment that one feels when Doctor Carver, with his humble smile, places his trembling hand on your shoulder and says, "Good-bye, my boy, good-bye. And may God bless you." It is a benediction from a simple, a kindly, a noble heart.

Clearly, this article was written in a time and place unlike the United States today, with different attitudes toward African Americans. It was a time when many Americans, particularly

George Washington Carver posed for this photograph sometime around 1906, when he was about 42 years old. Carver became a national figure in the 1930s, when his scientific innovations were widely publicized in mainstream news sources.

in the South, still felt that African Americans were inferior to white Americans and were not capable of working in demanding fields such as the sciences. Terms such as "Negro," which may be considered offensive today, were thought to be acceptable in describing African Americans.

Although the article praises what are seen as Carver's accomplishments, the author goes out of his way to make Carver appear as nonthreatening and harmless to whites as possible. Further descriptions from the article, such as "as he turned away to bend over his microscope, I heard him mutter to himself, 'God has been mighty good to this poor old Negro,'" which today seem tasteless and offensive, were considered positive and sympathetic by many in the more racially divided world of the 1930s.

Other articles soon followed. An illustrated story in *Life* magazine in March 1937 named Carver "one of the great scientists of the U.S." The *New York Times* praised his "300 useful products" from the peanut and said that Carver had "memorably improved the agriculture of the South."

After his death on January 5, 1943, the praise and honors continued. President Franklin D. Roosevelt said that "all mankind is the beneficiary of his discoveries in the field of agricultural chemistry." Just one month after Carver's death, Senator (later President) Harry S. Truman testified in favor of a bill to make Carver's birthplace a national monument, saying, "The scientific discoveries and experiments of Dr. Carver have done more to alleviate the one-crop agricultural system in the South than any other thing that had been done in the history of the United States." Carver received his monument, an honor that had previously only been given to Presidents George Washington and Abraham Lincoln.

DID YOU KNOW?

Did you know that the pioneering hip-hop group Run DMC paid tribute to George Washington Carver? The song "Proud to be Black" on their 1986 album *Raising Hell* includes the lyrics, "George Washington Carver made the peanut great, showed any man with a mind could create."

President Franklin D. Roosevelt made a special stop at Tuskegee to meet Carver in 1939. After Carver's death in 1943, Roosevelt praised him, saying, "all mankind is the beneficiary of his discoveries."

Biographies and articles written after Carver's death continued to praise him both as a man and as one of America's greatest scientists. Melvin T. Rothwell's *George Washington Carver, a Great Scientist,* said that Carver had "stepped out of the heart of the lowly peanut into the heart of humanity" and that his success was due to "a beneficent Creator who whispered secrets into his ebony ear." Ten years later, African-American author and poet Langston Hughes published *Famous American Negroes,* lauding Carver's "formulas in agriculture that enriched the entire Southland, indeed the whole of America and the world." (Apparently, Hughes was unaware that Carver kept no laboratory records and left no formulas behind.)

Carver became a legendary figure after his death. Not much is known about his early life; the statue above, located at the Carver National Monument in Missouri, is meant to portray him as a young boy.

Planted in the public's mind was an image of Carver as a man who was somehow the savior of Southern agriculture, a brilliant "creative chemist" who found hundreds of new uses for the peanut, the sweet potato, and other crops. It is safe to say that, even to this day, when you mention the name George Washington Carver, the first thing people think of is peanuts. Some even believe that he invented peanut butter.

Because of the popular beliefs about his accomplishments, as well as the genuine goodness of the man, the legend of George Washington Carver replaced the truth about George Washington Carver. For many years, he was one of the very few blacks to be mentioned in textbooks, a suitable role model for young African Americans. He became the first black man of learning to emerge as a folk hero to the entire nation.

Such mythmaking in effect clouded Carver's actual accomplishments. Carver was proclaimed a great creative scientist,
but that is not where his true accomplishments lie. Indeed, his
work with peanuts and sweet potatoes, the work that brought
him his greatest fame, is less significant than meets the eye.
His real strengths were as a teacher, a scientific popularizer,
a pioneer in agricultural education who sought to raise the
living standards of poor farmers, an early environmentalist, and a devoted friend who deeply touched the lives of the
many people with whom he came in contact. That he rose to
heights of national prominence had less to do with the reality
of Carver's life and career than it did with America's need to
put forth a symbol of black achievement—especially one with
such humble beginnings.

2

Obscure Beginnings

Carver's early childhood is shrouded in legend. His mentor, Booker T. Washington, said in his book, *My Larger Education*, that Carver "was born on the plantation of Mr. Carver" and "was allowed to grow up among the servant's quarters, getting his living as best as he could." Carver himself contributed to the story by calling himself "a poor defenseless orphan." This certainly exaggerated the story, but the truth itself was more than enough.

George Washington Carver was born into slavery on a farm near the village of Diamond, Missouri, during the waning months of the Civil War. His mother, Mary, belonged to Moses Carver, a frontiersman and homesteader who had settled in the southwestern corner of the state about 25 years earlier with his wife, Susan. Independent, proud, and thriving on their 240 acres, the Carvers were to be the only real parents George would ever know.

Moses Carver opposed slavery in principle, but his children had grown up and left home, and hiring labor for his Newton County farm proved difficult. In 1855, he bought Mary from one of his neighbors for $700. She was then just 13 years old. Records of the time are sketchy, but it is thought that during the next decade she bore at least four children, including twin girls who apparently died as infants. Two sons survived: Jim, born in 1859, and George, born, as he would recall, "near the end of the war," in 1864 or 1865. It is likely that his actual birth date was during the spring of 1865.

The identity of George's father is not known, but he was probably a slave on a nearby farm—a man who died around the time George was born. "I am told," the scientist wrote in 1922, "that my father was killed while hauling wood with an ox team. In some way he fell from the load, under the wagon, both wheels passing over him."

George never got to know his mother, either. They were separated shortly after his birth. Their parting was a traumatic event that reflected the horrific, turbulent times in which it occurred.

WAR COMES TO THE UNITED STATES

Missouri, a slave state that remained part of the Union during the Civil War, was a place of extraordinary tension both before and after the outbreak of that war in 1861. Governor Claiborne Fox Jackson was a proslavery man who favored secession, and a majority of the Missouri legislature agreed with his views. With the arrival of new settlers, however, considerable Union sentiment had entered the state during the preceding three decades, and secession from the Union was rejected by a state convention that was elected to consider the issue.

Jackson's subsequent attempts to claim Missouri for the Confederacy were thwarted by Union forces, and he and several members of the legislature were forced to flee the capital of Jefferson City. They eventually ended up in Neosho, only eight miles from Diamond and the Carver farm. After enacting an order of secession there, they were driven out of the state entirely and remained in exile throughout the war.

As such events suggest, the Missouri populace was deeply divided in its loyalties during the Civil War. In the border regions especially, guerrilla warfare erupted with a vengeance, pitting Confederate-sympathizing "bushwhackers"—including William Quantrill and the soon-to-be-famous outlaws Frank and Jesse James—against Unionist "jayhawkers."

The Civil War

The American Civil War (1861–1865) was fought between the United States (the Union) and 11 Southern slave states, which declared that they had the right of secession (officially leaving the Union) and formed the Confederate States of America. The Union, led by President Abraham Lincoln, opposed slavery and any further spread of slavery into territories owned by the United States and rejected any claims by the Southern states that they had the right to secede.

While state's rights, economics, and other factors certainly played their part in bringing about the war, slavery and the Southern state's claim to the right to own slaves was truly at the heart of the matter. The war raged for four years, pitting friend against friend, family against family, neighbor against neighbor, and brother against brother. By the time it was all over, over 620,000 Union and Confederate soldiers had been killed and many more wounded, making it the bloodiest war in all of American history.

With the war's end, the defeated South lay in ruins. Its countryside and cities had been ravaged by battles; its transportation system, bridges and railway systems had been destroyed; and its economy was in shambles. And it was now a society forced to cope with the liberation of 4 million former slaves, now living as free men and women among the very people who considered them to be less than human. It would take decades for the South to recover physically and economically from the war. It would take 100 years of struggle to fulfill the promise of emancipation and for African Americans throughout the United States to receive their full civil and political rights.

After the Civil War, much of the South's infrastructure was left in shambles. The colorized photograph above shows the ruins of Fort Sumter in South Carolina. The fort, a Union stronghold, was bombarded by the Confederate Army in 1861, officially beginning the war.

Ambush, theft, murder, and swift and bloody raids on farms and settlements were forms that the fighting took.

Union sympathizers like Moses Carver were prime targets for the roving rebel bands, and bushwhackers raided his farm at least three times between 1863 and 1865. On one occasion, in the fall or early winter of 1863, they hanged the farmer from a tree by his thumbs, burned his bare feet with hot coals, and demanded to know where he had hidden his money. Despite the torture, he refused to tell them and they left. They were more successful on a later raid, causing him thereafter to bury his money in various places around the farm.

Near the end of the war, the bushwhackers came again. Running from the sound of their horses, Moses Carver managed to rush the five-year-old Jim to safety, but Mary and the infant George were not so lucky. The raiders rode away with the mother and her baby and carried them into Arkansas, a Confederate state that lay 20 miles to the south.

A kindly man who had come to love Mary and her sons as more than just property, Moses Carver was determined to reclaim the abducted mother and child. To do so, he approached a neighbor named John Bentley, a Union scout who was knowledgeable about the guerrilla bands and their movements. Bentley agreed to go in search of the kidnapped pair, and within a few days he returned with George, nearly dead from whooping cough. He had been unable to find Mary, however, and what became of her was never discovered. For returning the baby, Moses rewarded Bentley with one of the prized possessions of the Carver farm: a racehorse.

Meanwhile, the long and bloody Civil War was drawing to a close. General Robert E. Lee, commander of the Confederate forces, surrendered to his Union counterpart, General Ulysses S. Grant, at Appomattox, Virginia, on April 9, 1865. During the next month and a half, the Confederate armies acceded one by one to their defeat. The momentous task of putting a traumatized nation back together lay ahead.

The end of the war introduced a new reality to American life: emancipation of the slaves. In Missouri, they were freed under the provisions of a new state constitution. As orphans of the war, Mary's two surviving sons were fortunate that the Carvers were inherently decent people. Having no children themselves, the white couple raised George and Jim as their own.

CHILDHOOD WITH THE CARVERS

Clearly, the loss of his natural parents and the circumstances of his early childhood affected George Washington Carver deeply.

As he told one of his biographers later in his life, "There are so many things that naturally I erased from my mind. There are some things that an orphan child does not want to remember. . . ." Even so, his memories of his foster parents were fond ones. The Carvers, he recalled, did their best to give him and his brother a good home.

Nonetheless, Carver felt a strong desire to learn more about his origins. He tried to ask Susan to tell him anything she could about his mother, but she always started crying when she talked about Mary. He often ran his hands over his mother's old spinning wheel, thinking of her. That wheel and the bill of sale for Mary remained two of his most prized possessions until the day he died.

Jim, the stronger and healthier of the two boys, grew up helping Moses with the harder tasks of the farm: caring for livestock, planting, and harvesting. George's recurring respiratory ailments, probably a result of the kidnapping, left him frail and sickly for much of his childhood, limiting his duties to helping Susan with tasks such as mending clothes, cooking, tending the family garden, and doing laundry.

Growing up near woods and wildlife gave George an appreciation of nature at a very early age. When he was not helping Susan Carver with the housework, he explored the woods and marveled at the rocks and the trees, the birds and the animals. As he recalled later in his life:

> I wanted to know the name of every stone and flower and insect and bird and beast. I wanted to know where it got its color, where it got its life—but there was no one to tell me. I do not know how I learned to read and write, but I did in some way, thanks to the Carvers. My only book was an old Webster's Elementary Spelling Book. I knew it almost by heart. I sought the answers to all my questions from the spelling book, but all in vain.

George indulged his fascination with nature by starting a collection of rocks, plants, insects, frogs, and reptiles. Susan Carver was not happy when George brought these discoveries into the house. After a time, she had him empty his pockets at the door whenever he returned from one of his visits to the woods.

Before long, Susan and Moses Carver recognized that George's curiosity and eagerness to learn made him special. From his work with Susan in the garden, it became clear that he had a particular gift for nurturing plants. He even began a little garden of his own in the woods. There, he transplanted and cultivated plants of various sorts, carefully observing the conditions that enabled them to grow and be healthy. He soon became known around Diamond as the "plant doctor," and neighbors called on him frequently to nurse their sickly flowers and plants back to health.

Closely tied to George's love of nature was a deeply mystical religious sensibility. He came to see the wonders of nature—not to mention his own special talents—as evidence that God was everywhere. As an adult, he was always quick to credit "the Creator" for whatever he was able to accomplish in the laboratory.

Exactly how much religious training George received in the Carver home is not known. Moses Carver was reputedly a free-thinker who distrusted organized religion and stayed home from church on Sundays. Nevertheless, George and Jim apparently attended the services at Diamond's nondenominational church, hearing sermons by a number of preachers of various Protestant faiths. By the time George was 10 or so, he had become a Christian. An integral part of his religious beliefs was a faith in divine visions. He claimed to have had his first such experience while still a child. Longing for a pocketknife, he saw an image of one in a dream. The next day, he ran to the spot in Moses Carver's field that had appeared in his dream, and, sure enough, the knife was there, protruding from a half-

George Washington Carver's interest in plants began at a young age; he was known as the "plant doctor" when he lived with the Carvers in Diamond. Later, Carver became a nationally known botanist. He is shown above at work in his arboretum.

eaten watermelon. This served to further his belief in God and his sense that he was meant to carry out God's mission.

Being such a bright child, George yearned for more formal schooling than he was receiving at home. His foster parents, although barely educated themselves, tried to provide it for him. The color of his skin, however, made this difficult.

Before the Civil War, it had been illegal in many states for blacks to know how to read. The new Missouri state constitution, adopted in 1865, mandated public education for blacks. Townships were required to furnish a school if the black population had more than 20 school-age children. For townships of less than that, the state government had no laws against "mixed" schools. In practice, though, townships such as Diamond refused admission of blacks to the "white" schools.

In 1876, the Carvers found a private tutor for George. It was not long before he was asking more questions than his teacher could answer. His spirits must have brightened when, in 1877, Moses and Susan decided he was old enough to attend the school for blacks at Neosho, the county seat.

THE QUEST FOR EDUCATION

Though his enthusiasm for obtaining an education may have mingled with the pain of leaving the Carver farm for the first time since his abduction, 12-year-old George set out for Neosho, making the eight-mile trip on foot. He arrived in town too late to find lodging, so he chose to sleep in a barn. As it turned out, the barn belonged to a black couple, Andrew and Mariah Watkins.

Like the Carvers, Andrew and Mariah Watkins did not have children. When they discovered the youngster, they were happy to give him a place to stay as long as he helped with the household chores. This lucky set of circumstances was made even better because the Watkins home was near the school. In addition, Neosho was close enough to Diamond to allow George to visit the Carvers on weekends.

Although obviously fond of George, Mariah Watkins was a firm believer in discipline and hard work, and she kept him busy. He even had to come home during recess to study and do laundry. She always encouraged him in his education, though, telling him, "You must learn all you can, then go back into the world and give your learning back to the people."

In addition, Mariah Watkins was a deeply religious woman who read regularly from the Bible. She introduced George to the African Methodist Episcopal Church, which was quickly becoming the leading denomination of black Christians throughout the South. Mariah Watkins's influence no doubt did much to affirm George's faith.

George's stay in the Watkins household lasted only about a year. The teacher at the Neosho school was a black man named Stephen Frost, and the range of his knowledge and his preparation for teaching unfortunately fell far short of George's hopes and expectations. George found once again that he knew more than his teacher did. If he was to obtain the education he desired, he would have to look elsewhere.

In the late 1870s, George Carver became a wanderer. He turned his sights to the nearby state of Kansas, which lay to the northwest and was rapidly becoming a magnet for Southern blacks searching for education and a better life. A family traveling to the town of Fort Scott agreed to let him accompany them, and thus began a new phase in his life.

3

Midwestern Wanderings

The move to Fort Scott, Kansas, in 1878 took George Carver, probably 13 years old, nearly 100 miles from his birthplace. Never before had he dared to venture so far on his own. When Moses and Susan Carver learned of his decision, he later recalled, they were "indignant" and feared for his delicate health. George, though, was determined to broaden his horizons beyond the little corner of Missouri he already knew so well.

After arriving in Fort Scott, the young Carver quickly discovered the value of the domestic skills he had honed in the households of Susan Carver and Mariah Watkins. In exchange for cooking and doing housework, he found room and board at the home of a blacksmith named Felix Payne. Carver earned spending money by working at a grocery store and taking in laundry from guests at the local hotel. He also furthered his thirst for education by entering school.

It was not long before Carver again felt compelled to move. This time, however, the circumstances that made him decide to leave were far more terrible than dissatisfaction with the quality of the education he was receiving. Rather, his stay in Fort Scott brought him face to face with a grisly lesson in race relations that haunted him for the rest of his life.

On March 29, 1879, a black man accused of raping a 12-year-old white girl was taken into custody and imprisoned at the county jail in Fort Scott. That night, a mob of white men stormed the jail and hauled the prisoner outside. With a rope around his neck, they dragged him through the streets, strung him up from a lamppost, and brought the public lynching to a savage climax by setting fire to the body. A huge crowd—of which the 14-year-old George Carver was a member—witnessed the brutal vigilante action.

Although more typical of the South than of the Midwest, this kind of scene became all too familiar to blacks during the next few decades. Whenever and wherever these lynchings occurred, the message was the same: White extremists were telling blacks that whites made the rules and that established racial boundaries should never be crossed.

Even many so-called respectable citizens approved of lynchings as way to keep the former slaves "in line." As the editor of the *Fort Scott Daily News* noted, "Had this been done quietly . . . no one could have been found to censure, but the unnecessary savagery of burning could well have been omitted."

Carver's reaction to what he saw in Fort Scott was to get out of town as quickly as possible. "As young as I was," Carver stated more than 60 years later, "the horror haunted me and does even now."

Fortunately for Carver, the next several years in Kansas brought him happier memories. He continued his education in Olathe, near Kansas City, where he lived with a black couple, Ben and Lucy Seymour. He then stayed briefly in nearby Paola before traveling 150 miles westward to rejoin the Seymours at their new home in Minneapolis, Kansas, in 1880. While attending the mostly white high school there, he made many friends who encouraged him in his long quest for knowledge. He supported himself by opening a laundry in a tumbledown shack in a ravine known as Poverty Gulch. In addition to nurturing his proven botanical talents, he developed an interest—and skill—in both painting and music.

One unhappy note marred these years. In 1883, Carver saw his brother, Jim, for the last time. That summer, George traveled by train to Missouri to visit Jim and the Carvers. Shortly after returning to Kansas, George received the news that Jim

Black Homesteaders in Kansas

When the Civil War ended in 1865, tens of thousands of newly freed slaves left the South in search of a place to begin their new lives as free men and women. Many of them settled in Kansas.

Why Kansas? One reason was a man named Benjamin "Pap" Singleton, who in 1874 had written a brochure entitled "The Advantage of Living in a Free State." This brochure, which painted a picture of Kansas as a paradise for African Americans, said exactly what many wanted to hear. Between 1874 and 1890, more than 10,000 African Americans moved to Kansas.

One of the towns they settled in was called Nicodemus, named after a legendary African prince who had also made the journey from slavery to freedom. Founded in 1877 by a white developer and six black homesteaders, Nicodemus was created to be a black community, governed by blacks, and entirely self-sufficient.

The idea of becoming part of such a community struck a chord with many African Americans. In July 1878, the first group of 30 brave pioneers arrived from Kentucky. The following year, 150 more settlers arrived, eager to start a new life in a free African-American community.

While they may have been eager to start a new life, for many, life in Kansas was much harder than they had expected. Pap Singleton's brochure had neglected to mention the ferociously hot summer with its violent thunderstorms and tornadoes or the bitterly cold winter accompanied by intense blizzards.

had died of smallpox. George, who had always been known as the frail one, would outlive his more robust and active brother by many years.

Although Carver declared years later that he had "finished [his] high school work" in Minneapolis, it is not clear whether he actually received a diploma. In any case, by 1884, he was out of school and on the move again. This time he landed in Kansas City, where he worked for several months as a typist and stenographer in the telegraph office.

Carver had hardly quenched his thirst for knowledge, however. In 1885, he applied by mail to Highland College, a small

Because the community was so new and wood so scarce, on their arrival the pioneers were shocked and dismayed to discover the lack of proper houses. They found themselves forced to make do in makeshift dugouts, really not much more than holes dug into the side of a hill, or even on the edge of a riverbank—far more primitive than any slave cabin. As quoted on the Web site www.inmotionaame.org, one of the settlers, William Hickman, recalled, "The scenery was not all inviting, and I began to cry."

Despite the numerous hardships, the pioneers were determined to stay and build their dream community. By 1880, 250 blacks and 58 whites were living in the town and surrounding area. Nicodemus began to receive nation-wide attention, and came to symbolize the hopes and dreams of the entire black community.

Unfortunately, the town did not survive. Blizzards in 1885 destroyed nearly half of the town's wheat crop, forcing many settlers to pack up and leave just in order to survive. Two years later, the Missouri Pacific Railroad laid its tracks some distance from the town, cutting off easy access to railroad shipping and transportation and greatly damaging the town's economic viability. With that, Nicodemus was doomed to fail.

But for the African Americans who left Nicodemus, returning to the South was not an option. When a reporter for the *St. Louis Globe* newspaper asked a woman with a child if she would return south to her former home, she replied, "What, go back? I'd sooner starve here."

Presbyterian school in Highland, Kansas. The college accepted him; however, when he arrived for registration, he met with severe disappointment. Seeing that he was black, the college officials refused to admit him.

HOMESTEADING

The degree of bitterness and frustration Carver felt at this setback can only be guessed, but it is clear that he chose at this point to put off his schooling and did not attempt to enroll at any other school for the rest of the decade. He remained in Highland for a while, doing domestic work for the Beelers, a white family who owned a fruit farm outside of town. Then, in 1886, he decided to try his hand at something completely new: homesteading.

In making this decision, Carver may have seen himself following in his foster father's footsteps. Moses Carver had built a good life for himself and his wife—and subsequently for Jim and George—by clearing and farming a tract of land in frontier Missouri. George Carver may well have thought that, by doing something similar, he could also prosper. Certainly, given his skill with plants, tilling the soil must have seemed like a logical thing to do.

Carver learned from the Beeler family about new settlements on the plains of west-central Kansas. One of the Beelers' sons had gone to that area some years before and had opened a store in Ness County. His store then became the center of a community named after him. Beeler, Kansas, seemed to Carver like a good place to make a new beginning.

The land in Ness County was subject to the terms of the Homestead Act of 1862, which Congress had passed as a way to encourage settlement in the country's vast unpopulated stretches of western territory. Under the law's provisions, anyone could pay a small registration fee and file a claim to 160 acres of public land. After five years of living on and culti-

In the mid 1880s, Carver decided to try an entirely new tack for his livelihood: homesteading. Such work was difficult and often not profitable for many years. The illustration above shows a settler laboring to plow his fields.

vating the tract, the homesteader could then gain permanent title to it.

Despite the cheapness and availability of land, supporting oneself by homesteading could be hard and expensive: Working the land required backbreaking labor and costly equipment. Accordingly, many settlers ended up selling their claims before obtaining the final title. Claims that switched hands in this way were called "relinquishments," and it was such a relinquishment that Carver purchased shortly after his arrival in Ness County during the summer of 1886.

Carver's tract was located south of the town of Beeler. His first task was to build a house, which took several months. During this period, he found work—and lodging—by helping another settler, George Steeley. Like most of the residents of Ness County, Steeley was white. It did not seem to matter to him that Carver was black, and, in the months ahead, Carver found acceptance within the entire community as he shared in the common struggle of life on the prairie.

Because of the lack of timber, the house Carver built was like that of many of his neighbors—made from sod bricks. He cut the bricks himself from the firm, grassy earth and constructed a tiny, thick-walled, single-room dwelling that measured a mere 14 square feet. It had a door, one window, and a roof made of sod and tar paper. He furnished it with a bed, a few chairs, a small table, and a stove. Nearby, he planted 17 acres with corn and other vegetables and tried—without success—to find water; he eventually resigned himself to hauling water from Steeley's adjoining land. In addition to doing what was needed to survive, he kept up his scientific interests by collecting local rock and mineral specimens and starting a makeshift conservatory of native plants.

Not content to keep to himself, Carver also took part in community life. He joined the local literary society, played the accordion (which he had taught himself to play) at community dances, and took his first art lessons from Clara Duncan, a local black woman who had previously taught at the college level. His white neighbors soon recognized him as one of the most gifted and knowledgeable residents of Ness County. Years later, after he had left the area and had become famous, he still corresponded with a number of people he had befriended during his stay in Beeler. In a 1935 letter to the editor of the Ness County newspaper, he wrote, "I want to say . . . to the good people of Ness County that I owe much to them for what little I have been able to accomplish, as I do not recall a single instance in which I was not given an opportunity to develop the best that was within me."

For all of Carver's attachment to the people of Ness County, his ultimate destiny was not in making a life as a Kansas sodbuster. He borrowed $300 in 1888 to secure final

Dr. and Mrs. Milholland encouraged Carver to pursue further education; they recommended that he apply to Simpson College in Indianola, Iowa, because the school did not discriminate on the basis of race. In September 1890, Carver arrived on Simpson's campus, which probably looked much as it does in the photograph above.

title to his land but chose not to stay on it much longer. The region's fierce weather—with its winter blizzards and summer droughts—made life especially hard, and it is more than likely that he found farming inadequate to satisfy his intellectual curiosity, not to mention his basic subsistence needs. In about 1889, he left Ness County and once more became a wanderer, this time heading east. He kept the deed to the land until 1891, when trouble with his loan payments forced him to turn it over to his creditor.

NEW FRIENDS IN IOWA

By 1890, Carver's wanderings had taken him as far as Winterset, Iowa. There, he found work as a hotel cook and once again opened a laundry. His religious faith took him to several local churches; at one of them, he met a well-to-do couple, Dr. and Mrs. John Milholland. His friendship with them was to be one of the most significant of his life.

The Milhollands, who frequently invited Carver to their home, were impressed by the breadth of his knowledge (all the more remarkable when one considered his erratic education) and his artistic and musical talents. They were sure that this young man, by then about 25 years old, was destined for better things. They helped bring his life into sharper focus by urging him once more to pursue higher education.

Carver may well have balked at the idea at first, remembering his unjust rejection by Highland College. The Milhollands, however, knew of a school that admitted students without regard to race: Simpson College, in nearby Indianola. With his friends' encouragement, he applied and was accepted.

In September 1890, Carver arrived on campus. His wanderings were nearly over.

4

A College Man

Simpson College was a small school operated by the Methodist Church, and Carver found its atmosphere warm and hospitable, although he spent only a year there. The one black student who had attended was gone by 1890, but the acceptance Carver received from his teachers and fellow students was gratifying. "The people are very kind to me here," he wrote in a letter to the Milhollands, "and the students are wonderfully good. . . . I have the name unjustly of having one of the broadest minds in school."

To pay his way, Carver turned to a tried-and-true means of support: He opened a laundry, working out of a little shack in which he also lived. His furnishings were so meager that some of his fellow students took up a collection to supply him with three chairs and a table. As he informed the Milhollands, they left these for him anonymously while he was in class. Sensing his need, on other occasions students slipped concert tickets or money under his door, never telling him who was responsible.

Carver's ambitions at Simpson were not focused on science. In fact, he did not take any science courses while he was there. Interested mainly in painting, he enrolled in an art class taught by a young woman named Etta Budd. As it happened, she was the daughter of a horticulture professor at the Iowa State College of Agricultural and Mechanical Arts, and it was not long before she noted Carver's botanical interests. Flowers were often the subjects of his paintings, and he sometimes showed her plants that he was growing. Although Etta Budd was impressed by his gifts as a painter, she feared that a black man could never support himself in that way. Carver obviously had similar fears, for he took to heart her suggestion that he transfer to Iowa State and pursue a scientific career.

The thought of leaving Simpson and giving up his artistic aspirations made for a difficult—and probably painful—decision. In the end, however, Carver reasoned that he could better serve the needs of humanity, especially those of poor black farmers, by becoming an agriculturist. As his letters of this period show, he felt a strong religious sense (which sometimes came across as arrogance) that he was meant for some special mission. "I realize that God has a great work for me to do," he wrote at one point. Scientific agriculture had obvious practical value, and, given his talents with plants, it became increasingly clear to him that this was the direction he should take.

BECOMING A SCIENTIST

Located in Ames, just north of the state capital of Des Moines, Iowa State was an excellent choice for studying agriculture. Chartered in 1858 with the land granted by the state government and centered in one of the country's major farming regions, it was among the first schools to give serious attention to research and education in this field. Carver could scarcely have received better training at any other institution.

Carver did not take any science classes when he attended Simpson College. Instead, he pursued his other love: art. He was especially interested in painting, a hobby he would continue throughout his life. Carver is shown painting in the photograph above; he was using a peanut-based paint that he developed.

Still, he had problems adjusting to the school. In August 1891, shortly after his arrival, he penned a homesick letter to the Milhollands, complaining that he did not like Iowa State as much as Simpson because "the helpful means for a Christian growth is not so good." Unlike the people at Simpson, not everyone at Iowa State was concerned with making him feel welcome. Some people shouted racial slurs at him during his first day there. He was not allowed to share living space with white students in a dormitory. Instead, the faculty converted an old office into sleeping quarters for him. Nor was he allowed to eat in the students' dining hall. He had to take his meals in the basement with the kitchen employees.

When Mrs. W.A. Liston, one of Carver's white friends in Indianola, heard about his problems, she immediately went to Ames to cheer him up. She strolled around the campus grounds with him and joined him for dinner in the basement. Although the dining arrangements apparently did not change as a result of her visit, he felt better about the place after she spent the day with him.

PARTICIPATING IN EXTRACURRICULAR ACTIVITIES

In fact, Carver's sense of belonging increased steadily over the next five years as he made many new friends and shared in a broad variety of campus activities. Participating in groups that ranged from the Welsh Eclectic Society (a campus debate club) to the German Club and the Art Club, he threw himself wholeheartedly into college life. He organized the Agricultural Society, arranged prayer meetings with other devout students, taught himself to become the first trainer and masseur for the Iowa State football team, and was active in the Iowa State chapter of the Young Men's Christian Association (YMCA), serving as its missionary chairman and, in 1894, as a delegate to the National Students' Summer School at Lake Geneva, Wisconsin. He also joined the National Guard Student Battalion (enrollment in the organization was compulsory for all male students), where he eventually achieved the highest student rank, that of captain.

Financially though, he struggled to get by, performing menial jobs on campus. He was not too proud to accept other people's discards—even other students' old pencil stubs for making notes on his classroom work.

Despite his busy schedule of activities, not to mention the various odd jobs he had to perform in order to scrape by, Carver did not neglect his studies. On a 4-point scale, his average in even his weakest subjects, history and mathematics, never fell below 3.0. His best subjects, not surprisingly, were botany and horticulture, in which his grades ranged from 3.9 to 4.0. He received his training under a first-rate faculty, which included two future U.S. secretaries of agriculture, James Wilson and Henry C. Wallace.

Carver became highly regarded by his teachers for his talents in grafting (uniting parts of two plants so that they grow as one) and cross-fertilizing plants (transferring the germinating cells from one plant to another). His undergraduate thesis, entitled "Plants as Modified by Man," dealt with his experiments in crossbreeding certain plants to produce hybrid varieties (offspring of a cross between two different species or subspecies) that were hardier and more attractive than nature's originals. His work in this area inspired Professor Wilson to observe, "In cross-fertilization . . . and the propagation of plants, Carver is by all means the ablest student we have."

Carver's gifts did not impress only his teachers; in one notable case, they impressed a faculty child. According to one version of the story, Carver was examining a plant on the college grounds one day when he encountered an unusually bright six-year-old boy who asked him various questions about what he was doing. Intrigued by the child's curiosity, which reminded him of his own childhood thirst for knowledge, Carver asked the boy his name and learned that he was Henry A. Wallace, son of Professor Wallace. After that, the boy often accompanied Carver on his regular walks in the woods.

The friendship between the black student and the professor's child was significant in light of what the boy later accomplished. As an adult, Henry A. Wallace became, like his father, a

While at Iowa State, Carver made the acquaintance of Henry A.
Wallace, a son of one of the faculty members. The two would often
walk in the woods together. As an adult, Wallace would become
secretary of agriculture and then vice president of the United States.
He is shown in the 1944 photograph above (center), accompanied by
Colonel N.S. Vasin of the Russian Air Force (left) and Colonel Russell
Keiller of the U.S. Air Force.

scientist, an Iowa State professor, and a secretary of agriculture.
He went on to serve as vice president under Franklin Roosevelt
from 1941 to 1945 and to run as the Progressive Party candidate for president in 1948. Wallace credited Carver with first
sparking his interest in plant life. Recalling the nature walks he
took with Carver as a child, he said that Carver "could cause a
little boy to see the things which he saw in a grass flower."

EXHIBITING HIS ART

Carver's abilities with plants were not the only talents to
bring him recognition during his Iowa State years. Painting

remained his first love, and, in 1892, he was encouraged to enter some of his works in a state art exhibition in Cedar Rapids. He hesitated at the idea because he lacked a good suit of clothes and the money to make the trip. Some of his fellow students then "kidnapped" him and rushed him off to a clothing store for a new suit. After he was fitted and the suit was paid for, they presented him with a ticket to Cedar Rapids.

It was a successful trip. One of the paintings Carver exhibited, "Yucca and Cactus" (a subject taken from the time he lived in Ness County), was chosen to represent Iowa at the 1893 World's Columbian Exposition at Chicago—a spectacular fair that celebrated the four-hundredth anniversary of Christopher Columbus's discovery of America.

Carver received his bachelor of agriculture degree in 1894. His teachers felt that he showed great promise and wanted him to continue his education. They also wanted to put his skills to use in Iowa State's classrooms, this time on the other side of the teacher's desk. Carver thus enrolled in the program for the master of agriculture degree and was appointed to the faculty as an assistant in biology, which enabled him to teach freshman courses.

He must have struck quite a figure on and around campus, with his somewhat eccentric habits of wandering through the woods every morning and of always wearing a fresh flower in his lapel no matter how shabby his suit might have been. His high speaking voice was sure to get noticed as well. Despite this, because of his remarkable abilities as a student and a teacher and his engaging personality, the majority of the white student body went out of its way to make him feel liked and accepted. One student later recalled a particularly vivid show of support for Carver: After Carver became a teacher at Ames, he frequently took his meals with the students rather than with the faculty. He was a great favorite with the students. One day, he brought his tray to a table at which a student who had recently come from the South was eating. This student did not relish the idea of eating with a black person, and he expressed his dissatisfaction by rattling his cutlery and scraping his chair, among other things. Finally, he gathered his tray with his provisions and went to an adjoin-

Tuskegee

Founded in a one-room shanty in 1881, Tuskegee went on to become one of the United States' best-known and most respected schools.

The school was founded on the basis of a political deal. W.F. Foster was a candidate for reelection in the Alabama Senate and approached Lewis Adams, a former slave, tinsmith, and community leader, for his help. What would Adams want, Foster asked, in exchange for his help in securing the black vote for Foster. Adams told Foster that he wanted an educational institute—a school—for blacks. Foster carried out his promise, and legislation was passed for the establishment of a "Negro Normal School in Tuskegee."

Its first teacher and principal was Booker T. Washington, who led the institute from July 4, 1881, until his death in 1915. The school rose to national prominence under his leadership, becoming the leading black institute of learning in the country.

Since his death, the school has continued to grow and prosper. The Tuskegee Veterans' Affairs Hospital, opened in 1923, was the first to be staffed by black professionals. The 1930s saw the establishment of the School of Veterinary Medicine at Tuskegee—today nearly 75 percent of all black veterinarians in the United States are Tuskegee graduates.

Tuskegee attained university status in 1985 and has since begun offering its first doctoral programs in integrative biosciences and materials science and engineering. The College of Business and Information Sciences was established and professionally accredited, and the College of Engineering, Architecture and Physical Sciences was expanded to include the only Aerospace Engineering Department at a historically black university.

From 20 students in a one-room shanty, Tuskegee has grown to more than 3,000 students in 70 buildings on a 5,000 acre campus. Dedicated in 1922, the Booker T. Washington monument stands at the center of campus. The inscription at its base reads, "He lifted the veil of ignorance from his people and pointed the way to progress through education and industry." To this day, Tuskegee aims to achieve his goals.

ing table. The students at that table had been watching. When the Southerner came to their table, they rattled their cutlery, scraped their chairs, gathered their trays, and went to the table where Carver was sitting.

As a graduate student, Carver was just as impressive as he had been as an undergraduate. Performing his work under the guidance of L.H. Pammel, a noted expert on plant diseases and fungi, he showed remarkable skill at finding specimens of fungus—a type of plant that lacks chlorophyll and reproduces asexually. He contributed hundreds of them to Iowa State's collections, and Professor Pammel remembered him as "the best collector I have ever had in the department or have ever known."

Carver also collaborated with Pammel on several scholarly articles and proved to be a popular teacher with students. In fact, he might well have stayed at Iowa State as a faculty member—which was what his teachers wanted him to do—if it had not been for his ever-growing feeling that he should do something more to help other blacks.

Two black schools courted Carver with job offers before he had even completed the requirements for his master's degree. The first was Alcorn Agricultural and Mechanical College in Mississippi. Although the salary proposed by Alcorn was no larger than what Iowa State was paying him as an assistant in biology, Carver gave serious consideration to the school's offer. He hesitated, however, largely because he wanted to finish work on his degree. Then, in late March 1896, a letter with another offer arrived from Alabama. It was signed by a man already becoming well known across the country as a black leader: Booker T. Washington.

JOINING TUSKEGEE

Washington had been appointed principal of Tuskegee Normal and Industrial Institute in Tuskegee, Alabama, when the school was founded in 1881. From its beginning, the institute's emphasis was on practical vocational training designed to help blacks gain an economic foothold in soci-

Booker T. Washington (above) was a leading force in the movement to improve the lives of black Americans after the Civil War. Perhaps his most important effort was his leadership of the Tuskegee Institute, which was founded to provide formal education to black students and encourage self-reliance.

ety. Agriculture was supposed to play a key role in Tuskegee's program, but for 15 years Washington had been unable to secure funds for a separate agriculture department. Finally, in 1896, the money for such a department arrived by way of the John F. Slater Fund for Negro Education, a philanthropic organization established by a wealthy Connecticut textile manufacturer.

In keeping with his general policy of hiring blacks for faculty positions, Washington wanted to place a qualified black person at the head of the new agricultural school. The Slater Fund trustees doubted that he would be able to find such a person. Accordingly, when Washington heard about Carver—who, unbelievably, was then the only black person in America to have received advanced training in scientific agriculture—he sought out the graduate student at once.

Carver did not immediately jump at the offer. It took the exchange of several letters with Washington before he agreed to take the position. He explained his hesitation by citing the offer from Alcorn and his desire to finish his master's degree.

Still, Carver was quick to compliment Washington on the work being done at Tuskegee and to stress his own commitment to the cause of black education. "It has always been the one great ideal of my life," he wrote, "to be of the greatest good to the greatest number of 'my people' possible and to this end I have been preparing myself for these many years." He believed, he said, that the sort of education Tuskegee provided "is the key to unlock the golden door of freedom to our people."

Washington, for his part, seemed determined to bring Carver to the institute and offered him a yearly salary of $1,000 plus board. "If we cannot secure you," he told Carver, "we shall be forced perhaps to put in a white man. . . . We will be willing to do anything in reason that will enable you to decide in favor of coming to Tuskegee."

Eventually, after Washington assured Carver that he need not come to Tuskegee until he had acquired his master's degree, the scientist agreed to join the staff. In his acceptance letter to Washington, dated May 16, 1896, he wrote, "I am looking forward to a very busy, very pleasant and profitable time at your college and shall be glad to cooperate with you in

DID YOU KNOW?

Did you know that while at Tuskegee, George Washington Carver lived on the second floor of a woman's dormitory? He was not allowed to access his room through the front door. To keep his living quarters separate from that of the women, he could only enter via the fire escape.

doing all I can through Christ who strengtheneth me to better the condition of our people. . . . Providence permitting I will be there in Nov[ember]."

After spending the summer finishing his degree requirements, Carver decided to skip the Iowa State graduation ceremonies and set out for Alabama in October. There, he would find a world unlike any he had yet encountered.

5

Southward to Tuskegee

Carver's journey from Ames, Iowa, to Tuskegee, Alabama, in the fall of 1896 covered nearly 1,000 miles. The significance of the move involved much more than the vast distance he traveled. The 31-year-old agriculturist had never before lived in the Deep South or among large numbers of blacks. Indeed, he had spent most of life living with whites and the majority of his friends and supporters were white. (Some people felt that, to the end of his life, Carver felt more comfortable among whites than with blacks.)

In Tuskegee, he was in the very heart of a region where blacks were numerous—outnumbering whites in many areas—and where a whole array of peculiar laws and customs were enforced by whites to keep blacks "in their place."

LIFE IN THE SOUTH

Life for blacks in the South was hard, and getting harder, at the time of Carver's arrival at Tuskegee. In fact, the turn of the twentieth century has been called the lowest point in the entire sad history of American race relations. The turbulent events that began with the Reconstruction period immediately after the Civil War and continued through the rest of the nineteenth century had brought about this sorry state of affairs.

With the South in shambles after the war, the North had to decide how to remodel the devastated and impoverished Southern society. Among the many problems to be dealt with was the fate of the former slaves. Not surprisingly, most Southern whites were far from ready to accept blacks as equals. Left to their own devices, whites granted few privileges to blacks and sought to keep them at the lowest social level—as slaves in almost every way.

Things began to improve for blacks in about 1868. The Radical Republicans—members of the Republican Party who had always been the staunchest supporters of emancipation—were in control of Congress, and, under their leadership, Reconstruction entered a new phase. The Radicals' programs included efforts to ensure that the freed slaves had civil rights. Measures were adopted to enable blacks to vote, hold office, own land, obtain schooling, and use public facilities. The local whites resisted these efforts, and often this resistance took the form of what we would now call terrorism. White supremacist groups such as the Ku Klux Klan sprang up, using violence and intimidation to deny blacks their rights.

Eventually, the North became weary of what was called "the Southern problem," and the power of the Radical Republicans waned and finally collapsed. Conservative whites in the South recaptured control of their state governments and congressional seats. Starting in the mid 1870s and continuing through the 1890s, whatever rights blacks had gained during Radical Reconstruction were steadily taken away. Segregation laws that separated the races and denied blacks equal opportunities for education and the use of public facilities were put in place and then upheld by the U.S. Supreme Court.

In an 1883 decision, the high court in effect dismantled the Civil Rights Act of 1875, which had outlawed discrimination in facilities such as restaurants and stores. Then, in 1896—the same year Carver went to Tuskegee—the *Plessy v. Ferguson* decision put the court's stamp of approval on the "separate but equal" doctrine. The court said in this decision that separate facilities for blacks were legal as long as they were equal to white facilities. In practice, though, the rule was "separate but unequal."

Southern states also adopted laws to deny blacks political rights. To keep blacks from voting, measures such as poll taxes and literacy tests were enacted. These laws capitalized on the widespread poverty and illiteracy of a black population just beginning to recover from generations of living in slavery. As a side effect, they eliminated many poor white voters as well.

Economic oppression was perhaps the heaviest burden that Southern blacks had to bear. The vast majority of the South's 5 million blacks were farmers. Although by 1880 one-fifth of them possessed their own land, a much larger number was still working on land that belonged to a relatively small group of white landowners. They were no longer slaves but tenant farmers.

The form of tenant farming that became a way of life for most Southern blacks was sharecropping. This system (which, again, trapped many poor whites as well) developed out of necessity. At first, it seemed to benefit both the landowners, who had no cash to pay for farm labor, and the farm workers, who could not buy or rent land. With sharecropping, the landowner could obtain labor by providing each worker with a cabin, supplies, and a small part of the acreage to farm. In return for farming the land, the sharecropper could keep a portion—usually half—of the money from the crops he raised.

Sharecropping proved to be an inefficient way to farm, however, and it was worsened by a host of interrelated problems that continually plagued Southern agriculture. These included an overwhelming dependence on cotton, a single cash crop that depleted the soil more and more with each growing season; fluctuating farm prices; poor agricultural methods; and a credit system that kept farmers perpetually in debt. In short,

Jim Crow Laws

Jim Crow laws were enacted in the Southern and border states of the United States after the period of Reconstruction after the Civil War ended. These laws required that public schools, public spaces, and transportation such as trains and buses have separate facilities for blacks and whites. In 1896, in the case of *Plessy v. Ferguson*, the U.S. Supreme Court upheld the legality of these laws, as long as the facilities or arrangements were "equal." The reality was anything but equal—the treatment and accommodations for African Americans were almost always inferior to those of white Americans.

These laws, enacted to keep whites and blacks separate and to keep blacks in a perpetual state of inferiority, touched on nearly every aspect of life. For example, in Alabama, train and bus stations were required to have separate waiting and separate ticket windows for blacks and whites. In Georgia, restaurants could serve either white patrons or black patrons— but never both. Also in Georgia, "It shall be unlawful for any amateur white baseball team to play baseball on any vacant lot or baseball diamond within two blocks of a playground devoted to the Negro race." And in North Carolina, "Books shall not be interchangeable between the white and colored school, but shall continue to be used by the race first using them." And in all Southern states, marriage between blacks and whites was illegal, and laws were in place making it almost impossible for blacks to exercise their right to vote.

When black soldiers returning from World War II were unable to accept the segregated conditions of the South, the civil rights movement began in earnest. In a landmark 1954 Supreme Court decision in the school segregation case of *Brown v. Board of Education of Topeka*, the court unanimously overturned the 1896 *Plessy* decision, stating that separate but equal was not equal. With that decision, along with the Civil Rights Act of 1964 and the Voting Rights Act, the days of Jim Crow, of legal segregation between the races in the United States, was over.

Southern farming was in terrible shape, and blacks were the hardest-hit victims.

As if dire poverty and the legal forms of discrimination were not bad enough, blacks also had to face the growing severity of white prejudice. By the 1890s, the South was full of white extremists who believed that, free of slavery, blacks were quickly degenerating into beasts who posed a direct threat to white women. These whites openly preached violence as a way to handle what they called "the race problem." Lynchings, which often involved an accusation of interracial rape, became commonplace.

The whites who favored the use of violence against blacks were not just those from the lowest classes. Some of them, like "Pitchfork Ben" Tillman of South Carolina, were among the region's major political leaders. As these extremists gained power, the quality of black life further deteriorated.

Such was the South to which Carver came. As he described it in a radio broadcast given in 1941:

> When my trains left the golden wheat fields and the tall corn for the acres of cotton, nothing but cotton, my heart sank a little. . . . The scraggly cotton grew close up to the cabin doors; a few lonesome collards, the only sign of vegetables; stunted cattle, boney mules; fields and hill sides cracked and scarred with gullies and deep ruts. . . . Not much evidence of scientific farming anywhere. Everything looked hungry: the land, the cotton, the cattle, and the people.

BOOKER T. WASHINGTON AND TUSKEGEE

In the midst of it all, the Tuskegee Institute was a leading haven for blacks, a shelter against the storm. This was largely because of Booker T. Washington.

By the mid 1890s, Washington was well on his way to becoming the most powerful black leader in America. Born a slave in 1856, he had so distinguished himself as a teacher at Virginia's Hampton Normal and Agricultural Institute (from which he had graduated) that he was chosen, at only 25 years of age, to head the black normal school at Tuskegee, which had just been established by an act of the Alabama legislature. Modeling the institute after Hampton, Washington skillfully courted Northern white financial support, sought to appease the Southern white establishment, and worked tirelessly to build up the school and its programs.

In 1881, Tuskegee held its first classes in a church. Washington then moved the institute to a newly purchased 100-acre farm that became the school's permanent site. Over the next few decades, with the aid of student labor and materials produced in the institute's own brickyard, one building after another rose as a campus was carved from the farmland.

Although Tuskegee was originally conceived as a training facility for elementary school teachers, it soon added industrial courses in trades such as carpentry and blacksmithing. When Carver arrived in 1896, the school's enrollment was edging toward 1,000 and the campus boasted 40 buildings. Carver was joining a flood of new faculty whose ranks swelled from 30 to 109 between 1891 and 1901.

In Washington's view, the kind of practical vocational training that Tuskegee offered was the solution to the seemingly insurmountable problems of blacks in the South—and many people of both races agreed with him. In 1895, while Carver was still pursuing his graduate studies at Iowa State, Washington had captured the national spotlight with a speech he gave before an audience of blacks and whites at the Atlanta Cotton States and International Exposition. The approach to race relations Washington outlined in his speech, the so-called Atlanta Compromise, called for blacks to put aside their efforts for political and social equality and to strive instead for economic and educational self-improvement. At the same

The Tuskegee Institute's original buildings were constructed mostly by student labor. Carnegie Library (now known as Carnegie Hall) was funded by philanthropist Andrew Carnegie; $20,000 paid for the structure and its furnishings, all of which were built by Tuskegee students.

time, he appealed to whites to give blacks a chance to advance themselves in the economic arena.

White leaders were hopeful that bringing industry to the South could lift the region out of its dismal poverty, and Washington played to those hopes. In his speech, he identified blacks as a workforce that "without strikes and labour wars, tilled your fields, cleared your forests, and brought forth treasures from the bowels of the earth. . . ." They were ready and willing, he said, to prove themselves as loyal, law-abiding participants in the building of a revitalized South.

Washington raised his hand high above his head as he reached the climax of his speech. "In all things that are purely social we can be as separate as the fingers," he proclaimed, "yet one as the hand in all things essential to mutual progress." Speaking these words, he dramatically opened and closed his upraised fingers to illustrate his point. The applause that greeted his conciliatory message was long and loud.

Washington believed that social and political rights would come for blacks only after they had proven their economic usefulness. For the moment, he was willing to make concessions to the Southern system, which did much to strengthen his leadership position, especially among whites. Many whites felt less threatened by and in fact eagerly supported a black man who seemed to accept the separation of the races. Partly as a result of this view, Washington's power and influence rose steadily from the 1890s onward.

Washington eventually created a "Tuskegee machine" that he used to spread his doctrines, advance the careers of those who thought as he did, and thwart those who disagreed with him. Before his death in 1915, Washington's racial vision and power-brokering methods would come under fire from other black leaders, most notably editor and scholar W.E.B. Du Bois. Earlier, however, at the turn of the century, Washington came to be seen by much of the country—black and white, North and South—as the spokesman for his race.

IN HIS OWN WORDS...

Upon accepting his position at Tuskegee, Carver said:

Of course it has always been the one great ideal of my life to be of the greatest good to the greatest number of "my people" possible, and to this end, I have been preparing my life for these many years, feeling as I do that this line of education is the key to unlock the golden door of freedom to our people.

Washington and Carver were very much in agreement in their views on race relations and black advancement. In one of his letters to Washington at the time he was considering the Tuskegee offer, Carver cited a recent speech by the principal and declared, "I said amen to all you said; furthermore you have the correct solution to the 'race problem.'" As one who had struggled patiently for an education and had been rewarded for it, Carver seemed to be a living embodiment of Washington's philosophy of black self-improvement.

With such agreement in outlook, the two men had high hopes for a good working relationship when Carver arrived at Tuskegee. As they were both to discover, however, the task of creating a new department at a struggling black institution would have more than its share of strains.

6

Satisfactions and Frustrations

The workload that Booker T. Washington placed on Carver after his arrival at Tuskegee in 1896 was heavy. Carver's main responsibilities were to administer the agriculture department, direct the agricultural experiment station, teach a full schedule of classes, assume responsibility for Tuskegee's agricultural extension efforts in the rural South, and manage the institute's two farms. In addition, he was expected to serve on various committees (including the institute's executive council, an advisory panel to the principal), act as the school's temporary veterinarian, supervise the beautification of the campus grounds, oversee the maintenance of the school's sanitary facilities, and even look into "the matter of reckless driving about the grounds."

The burden of these responsibilities taxed Carver's abilities severely. During the next 20 years, his talents, like those of most people, proved decidedly stronger in some areas than in others. The duties at which he most excelled were his teaching, his work with the experiment station, and his efforts to extend the benefits of Tuskegee's programs to poor farmers in outlying areas.

CARVER THE TEACHER

In the classroom, Carver showed a natural ability to captivate and inspire his students, whose educational background ranged from fifth grade through high school education but who in many cases were barely literate. To teach them was a definite challenge, and Carver met it admirably. Genuinely concerned with reaching his students, he was aided most by his great love and reverence for the subjects he taught. "Whether his course was labeled botany, chemistry, or agriculture," wrote Linda McMurry, author of a 1981 Carver biography, "what he taught was an appreciation of the miracles and beauties of nature."

An ecologist long before it became fashionable, Carver taught that everything in nature was interrelated. To demonstrate this, he had his classes study a single plant in depth and showed them how a whole variety of natural processes—chemical and biological—came into play to produce and nurture it. To Carver, understanding how these different processes interacted was the essence of learning.

One of the basic elements of Carver's philosophy was that nature produced no waste. Instead, what was called "waste" was simply failure to use it properly. To illustrate this concept, Carver would show his students a tangled mass of string that had been thrown away as useless. He would then show them a nearly wound ball of string, explaining that ignorance was like the tangled ball, whereas intelligence brought order and usefulness.

Always stressing the concrete over the abstract, Carver illustrated his points with plant and mineral specimens that he collected during his regular hikes in the woods and fields. He encouraged his students to make similar discoveries. For

Carver is shown working at his microscope. He was ever appreciative of the beauty of nature, and he passed that love on to his students at Tuskegee, many of whom had little formal education before coming to the Institute.

example, he had his botany classes compete with each other in collecting specimens. Such methods reflected Carver's belief that the student should participate as much as possible in the educational process. He felt that the teacher should be more than a "predigester" and lecturer of facts; the best teacher, in Carver's view, was one who enabled students to discover things for themselves.

Although Carver worked his classes hard, he was a popular teacher. The scope of his knowledge became so well known on campus that some of his students even tried to fool him once. On this occasion, a group of boys carefully assembled a fake specimen from parts of different insects and then challenged the professor to identify the strange bug they claimed to have found. Carver was not fooled. The insect, he declared, was most certainly "a humbug."

Carver's relationship with his students (he liked to call them "his children") went well beyond that of the typical teacher. From time to time, he loaned money to the needier ones, and, when possible, he tried to help students find jobs or further their education after they left Tuskegee. He also exchanged letters with a large number of his former students, following their progress over the course of many years.

PERSONAL LIFE

Carver never married, although he came close in 1905, when he apparently considered taking Sarah Hunt, the sister-in-law of a Tuskegee official, as his bride. The relationship dissolved, however, for reasons Carver was hesitant to discuss. He would say only that he and Sarah discovered that they had different goals in life.

Carver surmounted his loneliness with a deep religious conviction that came to play an important role in his relations with students. In 1907, at the request of several students, he organized a Bible class that met in the library on Sunday evenings. At these meetings, he linked his Christian beliefs with his work as a scientist. He talked about the way "the Creator" was revealed in the wonders of nature. Unlike many people today who see science and religion as incompatible, Carver believed that the two in no way contradicted one another. "We get closer to God," he wrote years later, "as we get more intimately and understandingly acquainted with the things he has created." Carver's Bible class, which he taught until his death, became a mainstay of Tuskegee campus life.

AGRICULTURAL RESEARCH

Carver's teaching and relations with his students were marked by an ability to inspire, and his direction of Tuskegee's agricultural experiment station was marked by an ability to do valuable work with very limited resources. The 10-acre station was established at the institute in 1896, shortly after Carver's appointment to the faculty. Its operation was financed by a meager annual allotment of $1,500 from the state. In contrast, the experiment station at the all-white Alabama Polytechnic Institute in nearby Auburn received $15,000 annually in federal funds as well as money from other sources. Whereas a staff of several scientists with different specialties carried out the research at Auburn, Carver was expected to do virtually all the work of the Tuskegee station. The lack of support for Carver's station was typical of how black institutions were treated at the time. Considering such limitations, as well as the multitude of demands on his time and talents, Carver's work at the experiment station was highly impressive indeed.

The basic purpose of Carver's station was the same as that of other agricultural research stations: to conduct experiments with different kinds of crops, soil fertilizers, and farming methods and to report on this research. The general aim of Tuskegee's programs in particular—to address the needs of an impoverished and oppressed people—when coupled with the limited funding, gave Carver's station a special emphasis.

Carver's direction of the agricultural station at Tuskegee ensured that he and his students could do valuable work, even with limited resources. Initially, it operated on an annual budget of $1,500. As time went on, Carver was able to get a bit more funding. He is shown working in his laboratory above.

It tended to deal with agricultural methods that were within reach of the poorest of farmers. "Even though his experiments were aimed at all levels of farming," Linda McMurry noted, "Carver spent significantly more time on projects that required hard work and the wise use of natural resources rather than expensive implements and fertilizers."

Much of Carver's research involved finding ways to build up the Southern soils that were worn out from too much cotton planting. This led to experiments with crop rotation, organic fertilizers, and various new crops that returned nutrients to the soil, such as velvet beans, black-eyed peas, sweet potatoes, peanuts, alfalfa, and soybeans.

It was important to demonstrate the soil-building properties of such crops, but Carver realized that farmers needed other reasons to grow them. Thus, his research emphasized ways in which these plants could be used to enrich a family's diet and to feed livestock. Carver's overriding concern was to help poor farmers improve their quality of life and become more self-sufficient. He encouraged them to depend less on costly purchased goods and more on products that they could produce themselves at little or no cost.

Carver wanted Southern farmers to grow crops other than cotton, but Booker T. Washington was a die-hard pragmatist who recognized that cotton would continue to be the principal cash crop in the region for some time to come. He insisted that Carver test cotton as well. Carver was reluctant at first, but finally went ahead when Washington allowed him to use nine additional acres for the purpose. In 1905, he planted several varieties of cotton, including a hybrid variety that he produced through crossbreeding.

Carver's hybrid produced good results for a few farmers who planted it. Unfortunately, it never went into widespread use. Carver's cotton experiments did gain some international publicity, however: Officials in both Germany and Italy sought his advice on the suitability of various types of cotton for certain kinds of soil.

Experiments with different types of crops represented one direction of Carver's research; experiments with methods of cultivation represented another. Carver was especially interested in testing organic fertilizers of both plant and animal origin, such as composts and manure, which were readily available to any farmer and would be especially beneficial to those who could not afford the chemical varieties. This interest typified his general scientific outlook as well as his concern for poor farmers. He firmly believed, he said, that "nature produces no waste" and that uses could be found for even the "lowliest" of substances. His later experiments with the "humble peanut"—the plant that became the key to his national fame—reflected this same point of view. Again, this interest in the use of organic materials and renewable resources demonstrated the strength of his vision as an environmentalist.

Carver maintained friendships throughout his life, and his friendship with James Wilson, his former professor at Iowa State, brought some benefits to the Tuskegee experiment station. After Wilson became secretary of agriculture under President William McKinley in 1897, Carver often sought the aid of Wilson's agency, the U.S. Department of Agriculture (USDA). Because Carver's facility was a black educational institution, it did not receive its fair share of the federal funds allotted to Alabama.

The USDA might well have ignored the experiment station, but Wilson tried to help Carver whenever he could. When Carver wanted to set up a weather station in 1899, for example, the USDA donated the necessary equipment. Furthermore, a number of Carver's experiments were carried out in collaboration with the USDA. During the next several years, he received agency support for a variety of projects, from attempts to cultivate silk to more conventional experiments with such crops as sugar beets, black-eyed peas, and peanuts. This support came mainly in the form of materials—seeds, fertilizers, and equipment. The Alabama legislature controlled the distribution of money from the U.S. government, however, and it made sure that those funds went to primarily white schools. For example, in 1912, the experiment station at Auburn received $69,439; Carver's appropriation was a meager $1,500, and it remained $1,500 as long as the station was in existence. Despite his best efforts, Wilson was unable to boost Carver's meager funding.

A vital part of Carver's experiment station work was the publication of bulletins that reported the results of his research. The bulletins produced by other experiment stations were usually directed to other agricultural researchers, not to laymen. In keeping with his aim to reach what he

Carver maintained a friendship with his former professor at Iowa State, James Wilson, throughout his life. When Wilson became secretary of agriculture under President McKinley, he tried to assist Carver in any way that he could, often in convincing the USDA to donate needed equipment for Carver's efforts.

called "the man farthest down," Carver wrote most of his bulletins in very simple, easy-to-understand language. Usually focused on a single plant or agricultural problem, many of his bulletins included practical advice, including cultivation techniques for farmers and recipes for their wives, as well as scientific information that a teacher might use. The titles of some of his bulletins—such as "How to Build Up Worn Out Soils," "Successful Yields of Small Grain," "Saving the Sweet Potato Crop," "How to Make Cotton Growing Pay," and "The Pickling and Curing of Meat in Hot Weather"—illustrate Carver's concern for practical application of his research. Because of their readability and their practical focus, Carver's bulletins were greatly in demand and widely distributed.

Neither Carver's research nor the information he included in his bulletins constituted anything close to a scientific breakthrough. Indeed, other experiment stations were performing similar kinds of research, and the agricultural advice Carver dispensed was hardly original. What made his work special was his concern for the needs of small farmers and his effectiveness

The USDA

The United States Department of Agriculture (USDA) is a U.S. federal executive department (or cabinet department). Established as a cabinet level department by President Grover Cleveland on February 9, 1889, its purpose is to develop and execute U.S. policy on farming, agriculture, and food. Its goals are to meet the needs of farmers and ranchers, promote agricultural trade and production, to work to achieve food safety, protect natural resources, foster rural communities, and end hunger both here in America and abroad.

In fact, while most people feel that the Department of Agriculture only touches the lives of farmers, its programs reach out and affect all Americans. For example, the food stamp program, the national school lunch program and the school breakfast program are all run by the USDA. All food safety inspection, ensuring that meat, poultry, and egg products sold in the United States are safe, is run by the USDA. The Center for Nutrition Policy and Promotion, which sets out dietary guidance materials, is operated by the USDA. Even the U.S. Forest Service, which administers to our nation's national forests and grasslands, is an agency of the U.S. Department of Agriculture.

in translating the accepted principles of scientific agriculture into understandable language.

In addition to his agricultural research and the bulletins that resulted from it, Carver sought to reach poor farmers even more directly. Under his guidance, the school broadened its agricultural extension programs aimed at raising the farmers' standard of living and improving their methods of farming.

Helping blacks outside its walls had been a major concern of the Tuskegee Institute from its beginning. Soon after becoming principal, Washington began to make frequent trips to the surrounding countryside. He knew more than a little about the problems of black life, but even he was shocked by the extreme poverty of the sharecroppers. He saw teenagers with no clothes to wear and families living in the single room of a ramshackle cabin, subsisting on a diet of pork fat and cornbread. On such trips, Washington talked to the farmers about ways to improve their conditions. Gradually, he developed more formal means of reaching them through the school's facilities.

FARMERS' CONFERENCE

In 1892, Washington invited about 75 farmers, mechanics, schoolteachers, and ministers to visit Tuskegee and discuss their needs. To his surprise, about 400 people showed up. After the success of this first "Farmers' Conference," he started holding such meetings on an annual basis.

Carver took over this program after his arrival and improved it. He used the Tuskegee experiment station to demonstrate methods of increasing crop yields to the visiting farmers, and, in an act of even more immediate value, he procured free garden seed from the USDA for distribution at the conference. Later, he supplemented these allotments with seed produced at the experiment station.

Carver soon saw that yearly meetings were not enough to meet the dire needs of the farmers. Following the model of a program that had been successful at Iowa State, he set up monthly meetings of what was called the Farmers' Institute. These meetings, which began in November 1897, provided specific advice about crop rotation, the use of fertilizers, and ways to restore depleted soils. In addition, the farmers brought in samples of their crops and had Carver analyze their successes and failures.

When the farmers' wives began to join their husbands at the meetings, cooking demonstrations by Tuskegee's senior women became a regular feature. In 1898, the Farmers' Institute participants held their first fair at Tuskegee, displaying what they had grown in their gardens and prepared in their kitchens. From one-day gatherings attended by a few hundred people, these annual affairs grew into events that lasted several days and drew thousands.

In 1904, Carver launched "A Short Course in Agriculture" at Tuskegee. Scheduled during the winter months, when farmers were least busy, the short course was a school for farmers that at first lasted for six weeks but was later cut to two. Carver and other members of the agricultural faculty instructed the attendees in a wide range of practical procedures, from the use of machinery to judging livestock, from organic fertilization to ways to make dairy products. Barely 20 farmers took advantage of the course during its first two years, but word about it spread steadily. By 1912, attendance at the course reached more than 1,500.

Carver was aware early on that extension programs that required participants to gather at a central location like the Tuskegee campus would reach only those relatively few farmers who were able to leave their farms for several days at a time. Thus, in his early years at Tuskegee, Carver assumed Washington's practice of traveling around the countryside and talking to farmers where they lived. Carver gained an even broader view of the needs and conditions of Southern blacks as the Tuskegee extension programs became the model for similar programs at black schools throughout the South. He soon found himself in demand as a speaker at such conferences.

In 1902, Carver journeyed to Ramer, Alabama, to visit a farmers' exhibition at a black school outside the town. The school had two teachers, Nelson Henry and Ada Hannon, who, while black, were both respected by the white community. But that respect only went so far. The two teachers received only $36 per year each for their work, and because they were black, were not allowed to live within the town itself.

Carver was accompanied on his journey by a white female photographer named Frances B. Johnston, a Northerner who was traveling through the South to put together a photographic survey of black schools. They were met at the Ramer train station after dark by Nelson Henry, who had arranged for Johnston to spend the night with a black family.

Apparently, the mere presence of a white woman among black men aroused the anger of Ramer's white populace. A crowd gathered at the station "to see what would happen," as Carver described the scene in a letter to Washington. He climbed into a buggy with Johnston and Henry and headed for the home of black family with whom the photographer was to spend the night.

After leaving town in the buggy, it was decided that it would be better for the photographer to stay in town with a white family, so Henry and Johnston returned to Ramer. There, Carver wrote, Henry

> was met by parties and after a few words was shot at three times. Of course, he ran and got out of the way (he fled twenty miles away to Montgomery) and Miss Johnston came to the house where I was. I got out at once and succeeded in getting her to the next station where she took the train the next morning. . . . I had to walk nearly all night . . . to stay out of [the whites'] reach.

Carver went back to Ramer in daylight to find that "everything was in a state of turbulency and a mob had been formed to locate Mr. Henry and deal with him." After Carver returned to Tuskegee, the institute launched an investigation that took the matter before the governor. Despite reassurances from the more moderate townspeople of Ramer, Henry and the other teacher at the school resigned their positions out of fear of further incident. The school itself was moved farther away from the town. In summing up the episode, Carver called it "the most frightful experience of my life," adding, "it was a very serious question indeed as to whether I would return to Tuskegee alive or not."

This racial incident, as frightening as it was, did not stop Carver from seeking to bring practical information to other farmers. In 1904, Washington hit on the idea of outfitting a wagon with various kinds of demonstration materials to create what he called a "moveable school" that could be taken out to farmers on a regular basis. The idea excited Carver. He drew a rough sketch of how the wagon might be outfitted and proposed a series of demonstration lectures. Funds for building and equipping the wagon were soon obtained from Morris K. Jesup, a New York banker, and from the Slater Fund, which had been established in 1882 to encourage education among black Americans. Tuskegee students built what became known as the Jesup Wagon, and a member of Carver's agriculture faculty became its first operator.

By 1906, the wagon was reaching nearly 2,000 people a month, and its success had attracted the attention of Seaman Knapp, a special agent for the USDA. At Washington's suggestion, Knapp agreed to put the Jesup Wagon under USDA supervision. Operation of the wagon then fell to Thomas M. Campbell, a former student of Carver's, who became the USDA's first black demonstration agent.

Carver's teaching duties, experiment station research, and extension work gave him much to be proud of. Through his efforts, the Tuskegee Institute had become part of a movement, and, indeed, was often in the forefront of early agricultural education. This success for an African-American school, despite extraordinarily limited resources, was a tribute to Carver and Washington. Although the lessons that Carver taught were hardly new, the straightforward manner in which they were taught, urging better use of natural resources, changed the lives of thousands of black farmers in the South. At the same time, his first 20 years at Tuskegee were a time of considerable frustration as well as satisfaction. The enormous demands that were being made of him were part of the reason. Certain aspects of his personality also played a role.

In contrast to his warm relations with his students, Carver never quite got along with other members of the Tuskegee faculty and staff. To a large degree, this was his fault. Arriving at the institute filled with high hopes, he was also brimming with a certain arrogance. Because Washington had practically begged him to come and because he held an advanced degree from a white college, Carver felt that he was unique and deserved special treatment. Within a month of his arrival, Carver was complaining about his accommodations, claiming that he needed an extra room for his scientific collections. The request for two rooms did not go over well at a school where a bachelor teacher was usually required to share a single room with another teacher. Carver did not make things any better when he confided that he expected to leave Tuskegee "as soon as I can trust my work to others, and engage in my brush work."

Such attitudes made Carver's colleagues resentful; other factors did so as well. His $1,000 annual salary was more than twice what many of the teachers were being paid. His Midwestern background made him an outsider in the eyes of the Southerners who dominated the Tuskegee staff. Even the fact that his skin was darker than that of the other faculty members made him suspect. In early twentieth-century America, as is still sometimes the case today, feelings of prejudice against dark-skinned blacks by light-skinned blacks were common.

Carver (front, center) posed on the steps of a Tuskegee building along with other staff for this 1902 photograph. Although Carver's relationship with his students was genial, he did not get along as well with fellow staff.

The result of all this was that Carver made few friends, apart from his students, within the campus community.

Carver's adjustment problems at Tuskegee might be traced to the special circumstances of his earlier life. Except for his childhood relationship with his brother, Jim, and his stays in the Watkins and Seymour households, he had lived and associated mostly with whites: Moses and Susan Carver, the Ness County homesteaders, the Milhollands, and the faculty and students of Simpson College and Iowa State. He had, of course, known white bigotry in various forms—the Fort Scott lynching, the Highland College rejection, the difficulties of the first few weeks in Ames—but these negative experiences were clearly outweighed by positive ones.

The white people Carver knew best never had anything but praise and encouragement for him. It is not surprising that, throughout his life, he seems to have felt more comfortable among whites than among blacks. It is also not surprising that this made it hard for him to fit in at an all-black institution such as Tuskegee.

The biggest adjustments Carver had to make, however, were to the demands of Booker T. Washington. For years, the Tuskegee principal had poured his boundless energy into building up the school, and he wanted the same commitment and discipline from his teachers and staff. When they failed to live up to his expectations, he was hard on them.

Washington was supremely concerned with practical matters. He had little patience for dreamers or dabblers, and Carver was both. Given a choice, Carver might have preferred to teach a few classes, conduct research at the experiment station, and, whenever he felt so inclined, take up his paintbrushes or go wandering in the woods. Washington, however, expected him to be a full-time administrator with the ability to pull a new department together and run it efficiently. Carver proved less than competent in this capacity, which required strong organizational skills.

Tensions mounted as Washington came to feel that Carver was mismanaging Tuskegee's various agricultural operations and improperly supervising the people under him. The institute's poultry yard, in particular, turned into a problem that would not go away. Under Carver's administration, the yard proved disastrously unproductive, and to Washington this was completely unacceptable. Not only were such operations expected to produce money, but they were also expected to enhance Tuskegee's image.

Carver became defensive when confronted with these problems. He had grown accustomed to receiving nothing but praise for his abilities in his pre-Tuskegee days, so he was easily hurt by any kind of criticism. When Washington faulted him, he always countered by reminding the principal of his heavy workload and his inadequate resources and personnel. He felt that Washington gave him too little support and relied too much on other people's opinions of what he was doing.

One of those people was John H. Washington, Booker's half brother, who served as the school's superintendent of industries and helped run things when the principal's ever-increasing activities drew him away from the campus. John Washington was no supporter of Carver, and Carver resented taking orders from him. As early as 1898, such frictions caused Carver to hint that he would resign if his working conditions were not improved.

Booker T. Washington recognized Carver's many talents, especially his abilities as a teacher, but the scientist's complaints irritated him. He urged Carver to complain less, swallow his pride, and do as he was told. Carver, on the other hand, felt that he should be left to the work that he wanted to do without interference, saying in a letter, "Now Mr. Washington, I think it ludicrously unfair to have persons sit in an office and dictate what I have to do and how I can do it. . . . If I thought things were to run as they have always been run I would not stay here any longer than I could get away."

Despite efforts to come to a fair compromise, the problems continued. Carver's ego was repeatedly wounded, and Washington's patience was repeatedly tested. Matters worsened in 1902, when a young man named George R. Bridgeforth joined the agricultural faculty. A bitter feud erupted between him and Carver almost immediately. Brash and outspoken, with organizational skills that Carver lacked and a strong hunger for power, Bridgeforth was soon convinced that he could do a better job of running the agriculture department than Carver ever could. He aired his cutting judgments in letters to both Washington and Carver himself.

Carver was outraged. As if Washington's criticisms were not bad enough, he was now being subjected to criticism by a subordinate. Forced to mediate their disputes, Washington often took Bridgeforth's side.

The troubled poultry yard became the main focus of the conflict. In 1904, a special committee investigated the operation and found it "in very bad condition." The man Carver had put in charge of the yard claimed that, on Carver's instructions, he had filed false reports about the loss of chickens and the number of eggs being produced each day. Carver denied having given such orders, but Washington's confidence in him, already shaky, was undermined still further.

Spotting an opportunity to rise in the department at Carver's expense, Bridgeforth and several other faculty members proposed a reorganization of the department that would relieve Carver of many of his duties, including his status as director of agriculture. A new committee was appointed to investigate Bridgeforth's recommendations. It concluded that the department's functions should be divided between Carver and Bridgeforth. Carver would become director of the experiment station and agricultural instruction, and Bridgeforth would become director of agricultural industries. This proposal was an attempted compromise that would assign Carver and Bridgeforth the duties to which each seemed best suited.

Carver's pride was bruised, however, and he rejected any redistribution of responsibilities or titles. He scoffed at the reorganization plan, rejecting the new title proposed for him as "too far a drop downward." He asked Washington to accept his resignation but backed off from this position a few days later. Instead of resigning, he demanded (among other things) that he remain in charge of the poultry yard. Washington agreed to let Carver keep his title and gave him a second chance to prove himself with the poultry operation, but it was a short-lived victory.

The feuding between Carver and Bridgeforth continued for another decade. Carver threatened to resign several times, and he did, in fact, seek out jobs elsewhere, even threatening to move to the African nation of Liberia, but none of these plans ever materialized. Despite continued problems and criticisms, he retained control of the poultry yard until 1913.

Bridgeforth also made gains, however, and Carver reluctantly gave in to two reshufflings of the department that chipped away at his responsibilities. In 1908, the department was reorganized in exactly the way that Carver had rejected in 1904: Bridgeforth was made director of agricultural industries, and Carver became director of agricultural instruction and the experiment station. In 1910, Carver got another title change: He was made director of the department of research and experiment station, a position that reduced his teaching load to whatever classes he wanted to teach and separated him from Bridgeforth's jurisdiction. Nevertheless, the infighting dragged on for several more years, and Carver was never really satisfied with the changes that were made.

Problems of this sort made Carver feel that he was not properly appreciated at Tuskegee. The constant feuding caused him to withdraw gradually from teaching and to focus his energies on research. It also led him to seek recognition outside of the institute.

As the success of his extension work put him in increasing demand as a speaker, Carver came to relish this public role, which, more and more in the coming years, gave him the praise and recognition of his abilities that he sought. By 1915, he was moving in a direction that would soon bring him fame at the national level.

7

The Road to Fame

Throughout his first 20 years at Tuskegee, Carver supplemented his experiment station work with research he performed indoors in the laboratory. Late in this period, he began to concentrate more and more on lab research while cutting back on other activities. His work in the laboratory ultimately became a cornerstone of the nationwide fame he achieved.

A laboratory was not part of the facilities Carver was given when he first came to the institute. Compelled to devise one on his own, he rummaged through the campus trash piles for whatever he could use. Old bottles and jars were his first pieces of lab equipment, and his writing desk served as a table for his experiments. He often referred to his laboratory as "God's little workshop," and every day he made a point of praying before stepping inside.

Carver's "lab," if one could call it that, remained primitive for several years. Not until the departmental reorganization of

When Carver first arrived at Tuskegee, he was not given a laboratory as part of his facilities. He pulled one together on his own, rummaging through campus trash for whatever he could use, including old bottles and jars. The photograph above shows his first laboratory, as it was exhibited in 1940.

1910 was Carver promised a fully equipped facility. Even then, equipment was slow in coming, and several more years passed before his laboratory could be called adequate.

Nevertheless, Carver made effective use of this crude apparatus during his early years at Tuskegee. He analyzed soil samples for local farmers to determine their richness and the sort of fertilizers that might be needed to increase each soil's productivity. Searching for ways to improve the diets of Southern farmers, he investigated various crops and plants for their nutritional properties, especially protein content. This led to numerous recipes using black-eyed peas, sweet potatoes, and peanuts, which he published in his bulletins. Intrigued by the clays he encountered in the Alabama countryside, he began to experiment with ways to produce paints and wood stains from their pigments.

Like his research in the experiment station fields, Carver's lab work was undertaken with the poor farmer in mind. Although he became involved in an effort to manufacture his paints as early as 1902—a plan that for some reason collapsed—he was not concerned at first with commercial applications. His focus instead was on products and processes that sharecroppers, rural schoolteachers, and other people of limited means could duplicate cheaply and easily for themselves. He hoped that having access to inexpensive paints would allow poor farmers to brighten up their often bleak surroundings.

In the later years of Booker T. Washington's administration at Tuskegee, Carver increasingly began to think of how the results of his research might be put on the market. He was responding in part to Washington's desire for anything that might generate good publicity for the institute. He was also trying to counter the criticisms of those such as George Bridgeforth and John Washington, who scoffed at his abilities. He felt that devising new products from crops such as sweet potatoes and peanuts was simply an extension of one of his earlier aims—that of encouraging alternatives to cotton planting.

CREATIVE CHEMISTRY

As his teaching and other responsibilities declined, Carver turned his attention to what was called "creative chemistry." In fact, during the 1910 reorganization of the agriculture department, the title "consulting chemist" was proposed for Carver, and he was ready to assume the role. Dreamer that he was, Carver had visions of creating a whole variety of products that would be instrumental in revitalizing the South.

The dream proved elusive. In 1911, Carver became involved in a second commercial scheme to manufacture products derived from local clays, and again, for reasons now hazy, the enterprise failed to get off the ground. At about the same time, some successful experiments with ways to preserve pork built up his hopes that meat companies might adopt his methods. Evidently, none did.

Despite such disappointments, Carver did not stop dreaming. He remained optimistic that, one day, a commercial breakthrough would result from his endeavors in the lab. Eventually, one of his dreams did come true—the dream of gaining recognition outside the walls of Tuskegee. His extension work and the growing number of speaking engagements that resulted from it made him a celebrity in regional agricultural circles. Although his products were never commercially adopted, several of them (notably his paints and wood stains) were used locally, bringing him praise and favorable publicity in state newspapers.

Typically, the praise that meant the most to Carver (as well as to Washington) came from whites. Noted English nobleman Sir Harry Johnson had toured the United States and spent some time at Tuskegee. In his book, *The Negro in the New World*, he made special note of Carver:

> He is, as regards complexion and features, an absolute Negro; but in the cut of his clothes, the accent of his speech, the soundness of his science, he might be professor of Botany not at Tuskegee, but Oxford or Cambridge. A European botanist of distinction, after ten minutes' conversation with this man, instinctively would deal with him "de puissance en puissance [as an equal]."

Praise like this, which might seem deeply condescending in modern times, meant the world to Carver. As Linda McMurry pointed out in her biography, Carver's early work, urging poor black farmers toward a more self-sufficient life, although important, had earned him scant recognition. Almost of all of the fame that he had earned came from white acceptance of his persona and the possibility of commercial development of his products. The basic human desire to prove his worth to the world proved irresistible to Carver. He changed his focus toward the commercial possibilities of sweet potatoes and peanuts and the hope for a breakthrough discovery that would earn him the respect that he felt he deserved.

DEATH OF A LEGEND

Then, in 1915, the first in a series of events that edged Carver closer to the national spotlight occurred. In the fall of that year, Booker T. Washington was on a speaking tour of eastern cities when he became seriously ill. He was hospitalized in New York in early November and then taken back to Tuskegee a few days later. All the while, his condition steadily worsened. He died on November 15.

Washington's death was a heavy blow to Carver. For months, he was deeply depressed and declined to teach class. He had greatly admired Washington in spite of their frequent arguments and undoubtedly felt guilty at having bickered with him so much. In a letter to one of the principal's aides, Carver wrote, "I am sure Mr. Washington never knew how much I loved him, and the cause for which he gave his life."

The death of Washington brought a new principal, Robert Russa Moton, to the school. Like Washington, he came to Tuskegee from Virginia's Hampton Institute; unlike his predecessor, Moton enjoyed genial relations with Carver. Moton respected the scientist and sought to keep him happy. Under Moton's administration, Carver was gradually released from his teaching responsibilities during the regular term. Within a few years, he was teaching only in the summer session, when refresher courses for schoolteachers were held. This, of course, allowed him to spend more time in the laboratory.

Another development that probably pleased Carver was the departure of his old rival George Bridgeforth. Apparently unhappy with Moton's leadership, Bridgeforth left Tuskegee in 1918 to become a county agricultural agent. Thus, although Washington's death grieved Carver deeply, it ultimately brought about changes at Tuskegee that worked in the scientist's favor.

In fact, Moton and other Tuskegee administrators found Carver a useful "replacement" for Washington. With Washington gone, the institute needed a star to attract both publicity and contributions. Carver increasingly fit the bill, and the school began to feature him and his work prominently in its various publications. This became another important stepping-stone on Carver's path to renown.

Carver enjoyed a double stroke of good fortune in the fall of 1916, when two prestigious organizations honored him. First, he was asked to join the advisory board of the National Agricultural Society. Shortly thereafter, he was elected a fellow of England's Royal Society for the Encouragement of the Arts. The second honor was especially significant in Carver's career. For a black American to be recognized by a British society was deemed remarkable, and newspapers took note; the contrast between his origins as a slave and his membership in the royal academy made for a great human interest story. (It seems likely that his friend Sir Harry Johnson was responsible for Carver receiving the honor.)

A year later, Carver's work attracted attention of a different sort. In April 1917, the United States entered World War I, which had been devastating the European continent for nearly three years. The resulting food shortages—a result of the disruption of trade, the diversion of crops to feed the troops, and wartime mobilization, in which able farmers and workers left their businesses to join the military—sparked the U.S. government's interest in ways to save and preserve foods and other goods. Several products and processes with which Carver had been experimenting, including a possible rubber substitute from sweet potatoes and a method for making bread by using sweet potatoes as a partial substitute for wheat, drew notice.

The USDA brought Carver to Washington, D.C., in January 1918 to discuss the bread-making process, and plans were made for large-scale experiments utilizing a device that could dry 10,000 bushels of sweet potatoes and help convert the tuberous roots into flour. Although this drier was not installed at Tuskegee, as Carver hoped it might be, the scientist was often consulted while the USDA experiments proceeded. The full potential of the project was never realized, however; the war ended late in 1918, and with wheat no longer scarce, interest in sweet-potato flour faded.

The government was not the only party attracted by Carver's work during this period. At the beginning of the war, a representative of renowned inventor Thomas Edison allegedly approached Carver with a job offer that reportedly included an enormous salary. Carver was always vague about the details of the offer, although some sources put the salary figure as high as $200,000, an exorbitant amount for the early twentieth century.

Carver said years later that he refused the offer because he preferred to stay in the South rather than move to New Jersey, where the Edison lab was located. The South, he proclaimed, had greater agricultural possibilities, and it was there, he felt, that he could do his greatest service. How much truth there is in the story of the Edison offer is not exactly known, but in the years to come it would become a popular part of the Carver legend.

THE POSSIBILITIES OF THE PEANUT

Although Carver's research encompassed several Southern crops, one plant in particular—the peanut—clinched his rise to national fame. In 1919, he developed a process for making "peanut milk" and enthusiastically touted its flavor, nutritional value, and capacity for use in cooking and baking. When representatives of the peanut industry heard about it, they were impressed with Carver's claims that the product possessed "unlimited possibilities." It turned out, however, that a method

The photograph above shows Carver working on an experiment in 1921. A few years earlier, it is said, a representative of Thomas Edison approached Carver with a job offer in Edison's lab, but Carver refused.

for making peanut milk had already been patented in 1917 by an Englishman.

Discovering this fact ended yet another of Carver's hopes for a commercial breakthrough. It did not disillusion the peanut growers and processors, however. They liked Carver's personality and recognized his value as a spokesman for their industry. Accordingly, the scientist benefited from their sponsorship.

In 1920, the United Peanut Association of America asked Carver to address its convention, which met in Montgomery, the Alabama state capital. Just having a black man speak at their convention was considered rather shocking, as the editor of the *Peanut Promoter* noted, saying that there were "doubts lingering in the minds of the audience as to the advisability of having one of the Negro race come before them." Even as the group's guest speaker, Carver was forced to observe Southern racial customs. To reach the upstairs meeting room, he had to take the freight elevator instead of the regular passenger elevator, which was reserved for whites only.

Once he reached the podium, however, he managed to dazzle the skeptical white audience, much as he had dazzled his students at Tuskegee. His talk, "The Possibilities of the Peanut," in which he demonstrated the variety of uses for the plant, was heartily received. An editorial in the *Peanut Promoter* noted how Carver overcame the audience's doubts and "verily won his way into the hearts of the peanut men."

A few months later, Carver dazzled a different group with a similar demonstration. In January 1921, he made what became a widely celebrated appearance before the House Ways and Means Committee. The United Peanut Association arranged for his appearance in the nation's capital as part of its lobbying effort on behalf of a proposed peanut tariff. Fearing competition from abroad, the American peanut industry wanted Congress to tax peanuts being imported from other countries. Carver, they felt, would be an effective proponent of their interests.

Originally given just 10 minutes to make his presentation, Carver wound up testifying for nearly an hour. With his usual charm, he presented to the congressmen many of the products he claimed could be made from peanuts. He demonstrated these products with a flair for showmanship that brought repeated laughter from the committee members. They craned their necks to see what he would show them next and seemed genuinely impressed both by Carver's presentation and by the sheer variety of the items he unveiled.

Carver capped his testimony by saying that the peanut had about twice as many uses as the ones he had just indicated. To that, Representative Allen T. Treadway of Massachusetts responded, "Well, come again and bring the rest." A hearty round of applause echoed through the hearing room as Carver started to pack up his wares.

Chairman Joseph W. Fordney agreed with his fellow officials that the scientist's presentation had been effective. "We want to compliment you, sir," he told Carver, "on the way you have handled your subject."

As it turned out, Carver's appearance before the House committee, which contributed to the imposition of a tariff on imported peanuts, did not charm only the congressmen. The publicity that came from his witty testimony marked the beginning of his rise to the status of a national folk hero. Indeed, his humor, his politeness, his apparent humility, his ready ability to engage an audience's interest—all of the qualities he displayed in Washington, D.C., that day—would capture America's fancy in the years ahead. Carver's testimony before the congressional committee brought him far more publicity and recognition from the newspapers than he had previously received. As stories about Carver began to spread, the Tuskegee professor was credited with almost single-handedly creating the peanut industry.

According to these stories, the peanut was an unimportant crop until Carver found new and diverse uses for it, making it a major part of Southern agriculture and helping to free the South from its dependence on cotton. The truth was far different. Peanut growing and processing already constituted a well-established industry when its representatives sought out Carver. Indeed, as early as 1909 the peanut was already becoming an important Southern crop: production grew from 3.5 million bushels in 1889 to 19.5 million bushels in 1909. When output exploded to more than 40 million bushels in 1916, the USDA called the phenomenon "one of the striking developments that have taken place in the agriculture of the south."

Also, most of the uses for the peanut that Carver demonstrated so compellingly in his lectures were not developed by him—and he did not claim that they were. In fact, as early as 1896, the USDA had issued a comprehensive bulletin explaining the value and potential of the plant.

Carver's work with the peanut did not begin until 1903, and it took several more years before he started to engage actively in creative chemistry to search for new products that might be made from familiar crops. His bulletin "How to Grow the Peanut and 105 Ways of Preparing It for Human Consumption" drew heavily on the earlier work of other agriculturists and did not appear until 1916, the same year that the USDA noted the growing importance of peanuts as a Southern crop. Nevertheless, because Carver was so effective in talking about the peanut, it was easy for the public to assume that he was personally responsible for all the many uses he demonstrated. What he demonstrated seemed marvelous, even if few of his "discoveries" had practical applications.

At nearly 60 years of age, Carver finally saw his name become a household word. Newspapers and magazines began to hail his genius in human interest stories, and a wide variety of groups sought him as a lecturer and as a spokesman for their particular interests.

In large part, Carver's achievements were blown out of proportion so that white consciences could be soothed. The white-controlled press manipulated Carver's public image to show that blacks in America could accomplish great things within

DID YOU KNOW?

Did you know that recipe number 51 on Carver's initial list of 105 peanut recipes led to the widely held belief that Carver himself invented peanut butter? The recipe, which was not original to him, makes an oily, gritty peanut butter that is a far cry from the peanut butter found in stores today. It wasn't until 1922 that Joseph L. Rosefield developed the technology for manufacturing stable creamy peanut butter.

the framework of segregation laws and widespread bigotry, so that no feelings of guilt were required by its white readers. Carver in effect became a token of black achievement.

Carver himself was guilty at times of pandering to the whites who turned him into a folk hero. Perhaps too concerned with gaining their favor, he seemed to accept all too readily the gross injustices of racial segregation, such as riding in the freight elevator or not eating with the white participants at a conference at which he was to speak. He never endorsed segregation, though, and if he appeared to tolerate it, he did so with the hope for a better future. A sincere optimist who frequently expressed a sense of solidarity with his fellow blacks, Carver held to a vision that a truly just and color-blind America would one day come.

Carver attained fame for work that today appears rather insignificant. His earlier efforts in agricultural education were far worthier achievements than his dabblings in creative chemistry, but they were not the stuff of which celebrity was made. The American public wanted to be amazed, and if that's what they wanted, creative chemistry was going to be the way Carver amazed them.

8

The Folk Hero

By the 1920s, Carver was free of most of the duties at Tuskegee that had burdened him during Booker T. Washington's administration. He continued to teach in the summer school, hold Sunday night Bible classes, and conduct experiments in his laboratory. His work in the fields of the experiment station, however, had decreased steadily since 1915, mainly because of his advancing age and a schedule that kept him away from the campus much of the time. He also issued fewer bulletins.

Finally, in 1925, Carver discontinued his outdoor research altogether. A new building was put up on the spot where he had once investigated crops and cultivation techniques. He still issued an occasional bulletin under the imprint of the Tuskegee experiment station, but these reports were few and far between.

Carver's research in the 1920s focused almost entirely on creative chemistry. He renewed his efforts to find commercial markets and producers for his products—products he hoped would transform the South. As his fame grew after his appearance in Washington, D.C., several companies, some as large and well known as the Ralston-Purina Company (famous then for its breakfast cereals), expressed interest in his discoveries and fed his dreams.

Because Carver cared little for the day-to-day details of transacting business, he asked a young man named Ernest Thompson, whom he had known for several years, to help him in these endeavors. An heir of a well-to-do white family from the town of Tuskegee, Thompson became Carver's business manager. It was his job to seek out potential investors and manufacturers and to help secure patents.

Early in 1923, Thompson arranged for an exhibit of Carver's products at the Cecil Hotel in Atlanta, Georgia. He hoped to attract commercial interest and financial backing for Carver, and in this he succeeded. By March, several prominent Southern businessmen, including a former Georgia governor, were planning the formation of a company that would sell Carver's formulas and processes to other firms, which would then manufacture them. The firm, incorporated later that year, was called the Carver Products Company.

In its four years of existence, however, the company accomplished little beyond obtaining patents for three of Carver's processes: two for paints and one for cosmetics. These were the only patents ever secured in Carver's name, and none was ever commercially developed. Thompson, as it turned out, was no more adept at business matters than Carver, and the other officers of Carver Products were unable to give much time to the company. Finding investors to take on its projects proved to be a tough—and finally insurmountable—problem, and the company died a quiet death.

Only one Carver product was ever commercially manufactured and marketed during this period, and it was not very successful. The product, an emulsion of creosote and peanuts

Carver is shown above in his laboratory at Tuskegee in 1940. In the 1920s, Carver began pursuing commercial research in an effort to develop products that he could patent.

called Penol, had been developed by Carver in 1922 as a medication. Creosote, a liquid distilled from wood tar, was widely used at the time to treat tuberculosis and chronic bronchitis. Carver believed that the peanut content in his formula added nutritional value to the medication and prevented the irritation and nausea that creosote could cause when ingested. His announcement of his discovery garnered him a great deal of publicity. One overeager newspaper account erroneously reported that he had developed a new cure for tuberculosis.

THE CARVER PENOL COMPANY

In 1926, Thompson joined with several Tuskegee businessmen to found the Carver Penol Company and manufacture the product. The sales were disappointing, however, and in 1932 Thompson sold the rights for the manufacture and distribution of Penol to a Virginia company. They did not have much success with it, either.

One of the reasons Carver never successfully marketed a product was that he was a restless researcher who often shifted directions when a new idea hit him. Throughout the 1920s and 1930s, his research projects were at least remarkable for their diversity: making paper from peanut shells, creating a synthetic marble from wood shavings, using cotton in a number of road-paving processes, and developing an artificial rubber from sweet potatoes. Yet his longtime dreams for a commercial breakthrough never came true.

Carver himself eventually claimed to have invented more than 300 different uses for the peanut. Carver's list contains many products that he did not actually invent, however, and many of the items on the list were simply redundant. For example, of the 105 recipes listed in his 1916 peanut bulletin, many were common kitchen recipes but later appear in his list of peanut inventions, including salted peanuts, bar candy,

IN HIS OWN WORDS...

"One reason I never patent my products is that if I did, it would take so much time that I would never get anything else done. But mainly I don't want my discoveries to benefit specific favored persons. I think they should be available to all peoples."

chocolate-coated peanuts, peanut chocolate fudge, peanut wafer, and peanut brittle. Carver himself acknowledged using more than two dozen other publications as the sources for his peanut recipes.

The list of inventions also includes 30 cloth dyes, 19 leather dyes, 18 insulating boards, 17 wood stains, 11 wall boards, and 11 peanut floors. These six product "types" account for 106 total uses.

Among other original uses for peanuts, Carver included substituting peanuts for products such as gasoline and nitroglycerin. These inventions remain mysteries because Carver never wrote down his formulas, and they may have simply been hypothetical proposals. These exaggerations of the number of his inventions as well as their lack of import or practical application cause most historians now to consider Carver's scientific reputation to be largely mythical.

Therefore, although the stories that circulated about Carver often credited him with creative miracles, few of his products and processes ever got beyond his laboratory or exhibit tables. Manufacturers found it cheaper and easier to use other materials and methods for making the kinds of goods to which he devoted his research. Most likely, he would have enjoyed greater commercial success if he had focused more systematically on fewer projects, working out their problems to the fullest extent.

It was sometimes reported that Carver's work was utilized by companies without his receiving proper credit, and Carver himself said that he was uninterested in who manufactured his products after he had developed the formulas. Carver was secretive about his work, however, and left almost no records aside from his three patents. As a result, it is hard to say what his uncredited contributions may have been.

Nevertheless, Carver's fame continued to grow despite his lack of commercial or real scientific success. The press, anxious to publicize a few black heroes, continued to exaggerate his accomplishments, and Carver usually let such reports stand without trying to correct them, at best issuing halfhearted denials such as, "How I wish I could measure up to half of the fine things this article would have me be." After so many years of feeling undervalued at the Tuskegee Institute, he cherished the widespread attention he was receiving and apparently was reluctant to say anything that might detract from his image.

A PUBLIC FIGURE

Clearly, Americans found in Carver a very appealing figure. In fact, his personality and public image were probably as important to his becoming a national celebrity as was his purported wizardry. In time, a particular perception of Carver arose— that of an aging, unassuming, and eccentric genius selflessly devoted to his work, his people, and his adopted region.

The public liked many things about Carver. His theatrical flair, his sense of humor, his sincerity, and his ability to explain his subject in simple but vivid terms were keys to his success with lecture audiences. His deep religious faith was also important. In his speeches and interviews, he almost always referred to the Bible and divine guidance. His accomplishments, he was fond of saying, were not his doing but were the work of God. As he told a reporter for the *Atlanta Journal* who questioned him about the permanence of the clay paints he had developed: "Why should they not be permanent? God made the clay in the hills; they have been there for countless generations, changeless. All I do is prepare what God has made, for uses to which man can put it. It is God's work—not mine."

Such words made Carver appear profoundly humble, and this image was supported by his lack of concern for outward appearances. Although he received many gifts of clothing, he preferred to wear old, threadbare suits, usually accessorized with a flower in the lapel. He could certainly afford better, but he was indifferent to money. Throughout his first two decades at the institute, he never received a salary increase; only in 1919 did Robert Moton give him an unsolicited raise. Stories were often told of how he left his paychecks in his desk for months until he was reminded that they had not been cashed.

Carver's fame and public image received an added boost when word spread about the purported Edison job offer. Although the offer had been made in about 1917, it was not well publicized until Carver gained prominence in the 1920s. Then it became one of the familiar anecdotes used to characterize the scientist. That his talents were recognized by Edison bolstered the idea of Carver's genius; that he turned down the offer was taken as evidence of his devotion to a higher mission.

Carver's renown depended largely on the various groups that gave him recognition. In 1923, two organizations with quite different aims honored him. During the March exhibit of Carver's products at the Cecil Hotel, the Atlanta chapter of the United Daughters of the Confederacy (UDC), a conservative Southern women's group, sent Carver a letter of "interest and appreciation" for the work he was doing. Three months later, the National Association for the Advancement of Colored People (NAACP) awarded him the Spingarn Medal, perhaps the most prestigious national honor given to blacks. Recognition by these disparate groups was a sign of Carver's rising symbolic importance among people of both races.

The UDC endorsement was a way in which Southern whites could show the rest of the country that their system of racial segregation was not so bad: If someone like Carver could succeed under it, it could not be nearly as bad as many people believed. As the UDC president claimed, "As a southern organization, we naturally feel an interest for the Negro that people of other portions of the country do not either feel or understand." In fact, the organization's response to Carver was typical of how many whites would come to feel about him in the years ahead. That Carver seemed so humble, devout, and uncritical of Southern racial practices made it easy to hold him up as "a credit to his race"—living

Dr. W.E.B. Du Bois, shown above, was a pioneering civil rights leader and educator. He founded the National Association for the Advancement of Colored People (NAACP), which later awarded Carver the Springarn Medal.

proof that blacks who worked hard could earn a share of the American dream.

The NAACP award was recognition by a group with a much different view of race relations. Founded in 1908 by W.E.B. Du Bois and others as an alternative to Booker T. Washington's type of leadership, the NAACP actively sought to change the way in which blacks were treated rather than to accommodate the white establishment, as Washington had often done. Although Carver's perspective on racial matters remained closer to Washington's vision than to that of the NAACP, he had nevertheless become a visible example of black achievement, and that was what the NAACP wished to honor. The implication of the Spingarn Medal was that blacks were just as capable as whites and thus deserved equal rights and treatment.

Carver rarely spoke out directly on race relations, and this probably made it possible for two very different organizations to honor him: Advocating a clear position might well have put off one or the other group. In making few public statements

W.E.B. Du Bois

William Edward Burghardt Du Bois (February 23, 1868–August 27, 1963) was a pioneering American civil rights leader, educator, and author of many books, including the classic *The Souls of Black Folks*. He was the first African American to receive a Ph.D. from Harvard University and was an early advocate of full equality for African Americans.

In 1905, he was a cofounder of the Niagara Movement, which, in 1909, became the National Association for the Advancement of Colored People (NAACP), one of the most important American civil rights organizations. Unlike Booker T. Washington, who felt that unskilled blacks should focus on learning a trade and improving themselves economically, Du Bois demanded that African Americans should achieve not only economic equality with whites, but full and immediate civil and political equality as well.

For decades, Du Bois continued speaking out on behalf of African Americans. In the 1950s, he often clashed with the U.S. government over his support for labor, for speaking out on behalf of the Soviet Union, and for his demands that all nuclear weapons be outlawed.

Increasingly disillusioned with capitalism and racism in the United States, in 1961, at the age of 93, Du Bois joined the Communist Party USA. That same year, he emigrated to the African nation of Ghana, where he lived until his death in 1963.

on the issue, Carver became an all-purpose symbol of black achievement, easily adopted by groups that differed as much as the UDC and the NAACP. On the rare occasions when he did address racial questions, he expressed the belief that all people were part of God's family and that social equality for blacks would come in due time. A firm believer in the Golden Rule, he said that he envisioned a world in which everyone would realize that "each individual, no matter what his color or creed, has his particular task to do in life." A persistent optimist, Carver felt that the power of love would ultimately conquer racial hatred and injustice.

Rather than address racial issues directly, Carver most often sought to get his message across by personal example. In his speeches, he usually confined himself to talking about his research, his views on nature, and his vision of a vital and productive South that made full use of its underdeveloped resources. He thus sought to open closed white minds by proving that blacks could think innovatively about matters of concern to all people.

Two organizations in particular gave Carver a public forum: the Young Men's Christian Association (YMCA) and the Commission on Interracial Cooperation (CIC), based in Atlanta. After World War I, amid heightened racial tensions, these two groups began to work together to promote a dialog between blacks and whites. The CIC, a moderate body that had the blessing of the Tuskegee Institute, was seeking black speakers to address white audiences, and Carver's rising renown, eloquence, and proven success with white listeners made him a natural choice.

In 1923, the CIC leadership arranged for Carver to address white college students attending a YMCA summer regional conference at Blue Ridge, North Carolina. As he spoke to the group about the wondrous resources of nature and how they might be utilized for the good of humanity, he noticed among the crowd a young man who seemed especially attentive. After the speech, they met. The young man's name was Jimmie Hardwick, and when he told Carver that he wanted to talk to him further, Carver declared, "Of course! I'd like you for one of my boys."

Hardwick was not sure what Carver meant by the remark, but two days later he found out. A lifelong bachelor, Carver explained that, when he formed friendships with young people who were receptive to his message, he thought of them as his adopted children. "In my work," he told Hardwick, "I meet many young people who are seeking truth. God has given me some knowledge. When they will let me, I try to pass it on to my boys." Hardwick, a Virginian descended from slave owners, was moved. "I'd like to be one of your boys, Professor Carver, if you will have me," he said.

There were to be many like Jimmie Hardwick over the years. Everywhere Carver spoke—at colleges, meetings of religious organizations, and other YMCA conferences, among other places—he found new "children" for his "family." Just as he had done with his former Tuskegee students, he often initiated correspondence that lasted for years. The letters exchanged between Carver and his "children" were usually filled with emotion and mutual affection. Carver was enormously fond of young people, and in turn they often idolized him and saw him as a true friend and mentor. In many cases, it is clear that Carver's personal example did indeed change minds that had previously held to prejudiced notions of black inferiority. "You have shown me the one race, the human race," one of his boys wrote. "Color of skin or form of hair mean nothing to me now."

One of the more dramatic instances of Carver's ability to promote interracial goodwill occurred in 1924, when he returned to the Blue Ridge conference. As a racial protest, the white delegations from Florida and Louisiana had planned to walk out during Carver's lecture. The Tuskegee professor so captivated the gathering, however, that the walkout never materialized.

When Carver was finished, the leader of the Florida group stood up and apologized to him for what he and the others had planned to do. During the next few days, Carver was besieged by dozens of students who wanted to meet him. Many invited him to speak at their campuses, and many more joined his "family."

For many of his white audiences, hearing Carver, an educated black man, was a true eye opener. As a report from Clemson College pointed out, "To see a man as black as Doctor Carver and yet as able as he is, comes as a distinct shock to Southern boys, and jars them of their conviction of the negro's absolute inferiority."

Following Carver's example, a number of young people he came to know played roles in the cause of better race relations. Jimmie Hardwick, for one, remained active in the YMCA and helped arrange some of Carver's later tours. Another young man, Howard Kester, combined his Christian beliefs with socialist convictions and worked actively to promote racial justice. With his life frequently threatened by white supremacists, Kester investigated lynchings and helped to organize sharecroppers of both races into a union. Like Hardwick, he remained a close friend of Carver's until the professor's death.

Late in 1924, one of Carver's speaking appearances had repercussions that he did not anticipate. In November, he made his first trip to New York City, where he addressed a meeting of the Women's Board of Domestic Missions of the Reformed Church in America. Before a crowd of 500 at the Marble Collegiate Church, he spoke on a theme dear to him: the relationship between his scientific work and his religious faith. He told the audience that he relied on divine inspiration in his research. "No books ever go into my laboratory," he declared.

"I never have to grope for methods. The method is revealed at the moment I am inspired to create something new."

The audience applauded heartily, but two days later a different reaction to his speech appeared in a *New York Times* editorial. Entitled "Men of Science Never Talk That Way," the editorial said that Carver's words showed a deplorable disregard for the accepted methods of science. The editorial argued that, by "scorning" books and attributing his success to inspiration, Carver was inviting ridicule on "an admirable institution [Tuskegee] and the race for which it has done and is still doing so much."

Deeply hurt, Carver penned a reply to the *Times*, asserting that his message had been misinterpreted. "Inspiration is never at variance with information," he wrote. "In fact, the more information one has, the greater will be the inspiration." He summarized his academic credentials and included a lengthy list of the scientists whose books he had studied. Carver argued that books were primarily of use to the scientist who was not already "a master of analytical work." He declared that a "master analyst"—a category in which he apparently included himself—needed no book but was "at liberty to take apart and put together substances to suit his particular taste or fancy."

Carver closed his reply with an example of what he meant by inspiration. He described how, during his visit to New York, he had been struck by the exotic edible roots being sold in the city's vegetable markets:

> Just as soon as I saw these luscious roots, I marveled at the wonderful possibilities for their expansion. Dozens of things came to me while standing there looking at them. I would follow the same or similar lines I have pursued in developing products from the white potato. I know of no one who has worked with these roots in this way. I know of no book from which I can get this information, yet I will have no trouble in doing it.

If this is not inspiration and information from a source
greater than myself, or greater than anyone has wrought up
to the present time, kindly tell me what it is.

The *Times* did not print Carver's letter, but many of Carver's
friends came to his defense. They circulated copies of his reply,
and a number of other newspapers picked it up. In fact, so
many people came forward to reassure and defend him that he
finally decided the controversy was, in the end, a good thing.

The *Times*, though, had a legitimate point. To the extent
that Carver relied on divine inspiration in his work, his methods were unorthodox and unscientific. It is doubtful that very
many other scientists, even religious scientists, would wholeheartedly endorse such an approach. Among religious groups,
however, Carver's statements were endearing and enhanced his
image all the more.

For the rest of the 1920s and well into the 1930s, Carver's
fame continued to grow. He remained a popular speaker with
student audiences, touring white colleges throughout the
South and elsewhere. In addition, he continued to appear at
farmer's conferences, black schools, and state fairs, as well as
gatherings of civic clubs, NAACP chapters, and other groups.
In 1928, Simpson College (his first alma mater) gave him an
honorary doctor of science degree—another award in what
was to become, by the time of his death, a long string of honors. (The honorary doctorate was especially pleasing because
many people had been mistakenly calling him "Dr. Carver"
for years.)

The peanut industry, which had been instrumental in
Carver's rise to prominence, continued to use him as a publi-
cist and to give him publicity in return. Its trade publications,
most notably *The Peanut Journal*, carried dozens of his articles
and also printed numerous pieces about him, declaring that
"Professor Carver is to the peanut industry what Edison is
to electricity." Such exposure fixed Carver in the public mind

as the "Peanut Man" although his research with this plant decreased after 1924.

Carver's experimental work rarely involved peanuts at that time, but his peanut expertise was still in demand. The Tom Huston Peanut Company of Columbus, Georgia, a peanut processor well known for its product Tom's Peanuts, consulted Carver on a regular basis about a variety of technical problems and even offered him a job on its research staff in 1929. Although he declined the offer, he continued to aid the company—without pay—for several more years. In fact, a year after making the job offer, the firm asked him to tackle one of the thorniest problems it had ever faced.

In the spring of 1930, the company had asked several farmers in Alabama, Georgia, and Florida to experiment with two varieties of Virginia peanuts, hoping to determine whether such types could be grown successfully in the lower South. When a sizable portion of the experimental crops failed, company officials suspected plant disease. They consulted scientists at several agricultural stations in the three states, and most said that disease was not a key factor in the crop failure.

Skeptical of what the scientists were saying, the company turned to Carver, who conducted his own investigation and identified fungal infections as a major source of the problem. Although Carver had studied such plant diseases as a graduate student and had collected and identified many fungus specimens over the years, he certainly was not a specialist in this field of research. Nevertheless, when the USDA was finally brought in to investigate on its own, Carver's findings proved to be remarkably accurate. The talents that had impressed his Iowa State professors many years before were undiminished.

Paul R. Miller, the scientist who conducted the USDA investigation, became friendly with Carver and encouraged him to send whatever fungus specimens he discovered to other USDA researchers. Carver did so, and his findings turned up several new species as well as varieties that had not been previously seen in the United States. In 1935, the USDA recognized Carver's work by appointing him a collaborator in its Mycology and Plant Disease Survey.

This episode shows one direction Carver's career might have taken if he had chosen to remain at Iowa State in 1896 rather than to join the Tuskegee faculty. He might well have obtained a Ph.D. in botany (something he had always wanted to do but that his Tuskegee workload had not permitted) and done significant research on plant diseases. Such a specialized career likely would not have made him a public figure, however. As things turned out, he became a well-known scientist even though his scientific skills were applied to projects that bore no real fruit.

9

Beyond the Legend

In the early 1930s, Carver achieved an even greater degree of fame. The awards were as plentiful as ever, the requests for speaking appearances unceasing, and the press attention nearly always favorable. Then, in 1932, James Saxon Childers's article was published in *American Magazine,* and it had an enormous impact on the Carver legend.

Entitled "A Boy Who Was Traded for a Horse," the story helped spread the myth that Carver had all but created the peanut industry, and it played up his image as a kindly, humble eccentric, shuffling along the Alabama back roads in a patch-covered coat. There had been many articles about Carver before, but this one was probably the most widely read. After it was published, Carver's mailbox was flooded with letters—a response that was repeated five years later when *Reader's Digest* reprinted the article.

In 1933, another article added a new dimension to the Carver legend, bringing to light an area of his work not widely publicized before. The Associated Press, a news agency whose stories are carried by hundreds of newspapers, produced an article that suggested that Carver had developed a new therapy for treating people crippled by polio. This story not only buttressed Carver's fame, it also brought a stream of polio victims to Tuskegee to seek Carver's help.

Peanut oil massages were the basis of Carver's therapy, for he believed that the nutritive properties of the oil could restore withered tissues. He reached this conclusion in the 1920s, he said, when some women using one of his cosmetic products complained that the lotion made their faces look fat. Apparently, the peanut oil contained in the product caused the skin to expand as it was absorbed.

This led Carver to try massages with peanut oil on a frail, anemic Tuskegee boy. The boy gained 30 pounds in the course of a month, and Carver was sure he was on the brink of a major breakthrough. He believed that the oil's nutrients had entered the bloodstream through absorption into the skin and, almost miraculously, had given the boy improved health.

Carver later tried his peanut oil massages on two polio patients. Again, the results were impressive, and, after the Associated Press story broke, Carver was besieged with requests for help. A number of people wrote to him, and many others got into their cars and drove to see him at Tuskegee.

In 1934, Carver started to devote his weekends to treating selected patients with his massage therapy. From this work came dozens of testimonials to the success of his treatments, and a number of doctors tried his procedures. Carver saw the results he achieved as one more example of how God worked through him. "Truly," he wrote to a friend, "God is speaking through these peanut oils I am working with. Marvelous, some come to me on crutches, canes, etc. and in time go away walking."

Despite Carver's conviction that the peanut oils were the key to his patients' recovery, it is much more likely that the other features of his therapy—expert massage and a regimen of exercise and hot salt baths—were the real remedies. Carver had been a skillful masseur since his days as a trainer for the Iowa State football team, and what he did with his hands was probably far more effective than the type of oil he used. Although at least one prominent doctor thought the peanut oil might have special value, the medical profession as a whole remained skeptical.

USING SCIENCE FOR PROBLEM SOLVING

At the same time that his massage therapy was sending him in a new direction, Carver was returning to some of his older concerns. In the early 1930s, with the country in the midst of the Great Depression, he returned to many of the goals of his earliest research and teaching. He became less concerned with the commercial potential of creative chemistry; instead, he began to reemphasize the importance of diet, nutrition, and economical ways to feed one's family.

Carver's commercial failures of the previous years may have been one of the reasons why he chose to refocus his work, but the hard times besetting the country were obviously the key factor. The dire state of the economy discouraged new commercial ventures, and, with so many people out of work and going hungry, he again saw the need to encourage self-sufficiency and ways to make the best use of available resources. He therefore wrote articles and pamphlets on possible solutions to the hunger problem, contributed dozens of recipes to various publications, and issued bulletins on natural fertilizers and raising livestock.

In 1935, a philanthropic grant enabled the institute to hire an assistant for Carver, whose age and declining health were draining his energies. Austin Curtis, a young man with a chemistry degree from Cornell University, got the job. Carver

In 1937, Carver addressed a chemurgic conference in Dearborn, Michigan, where he met automobile manufacturer Henry Ford. The two immediately became good friends; they are shown above, talking in Ford's foods laboratory in 1942.

came to think of Curtis as a son. He helped the professor with his research and took on some projects of his own. After so many years of working alone, Carver finally had an assistant at just the point when his laboratory work was drawing to a close.

While his "real work" declined, Carver's value as a symbol continued to rise. The most significant new group to adopt him during the 1930s was the so-called chemurgic movement. Through its journal and national council, this group sought to promote research "in Chemistry and related Sciences" that would aid agriculture by using raw agricultural materials to develop new industrial chemical products—precisely the kind of work Carver had been doing for decades.

In 1937, Carver addressed three different chemurgic conferences. At the meeting in Dearborn, Michigan, he met the movement's most well-known sponsor: auto manufacturer Henry Ford. Carver and the industrial giant immediately became good friends. Between the time of their first meeting and Carver's death, they visited each other on several occasions and exchanged letters. Recognition by prominent whites meant much to Carver, and he was especially proud to know Ford. In one letter, Carver told him, "I consider you the greatest man I have ever met."

Also in 1937, Carver was honored at a Tuskegee celebration that marked his 40 years of service to the institute. The ceremonies included the unveiling of a bronze bust of Carver and a speech by H.E. Barnard, director of the Farm Chemurgic Council. In his address, Barnard praised Carver's early research for anticipating much of what was currently being done in the field. The celebration was highly publicized in national magazines and in newspapers throughout the country. Additional recognition came that same year when the National Technical Association and the Mark Twain Society each made Carver an honorary member of their groups.

By then, Carver had begun to appear on a number of nationally broadcast radio programs, including *It Can Be Done* and *We the People*. The Smithsonian Institution produced a series of broadcasts that chronicled his life story; other radio programs also detailed his life. The cumulative effect of these profiles enhanced his reputation even further.

Carver's fame was heightened in 1938 when his life received the "Hollywood treatment." His career was depicted in a short film called *The Story of Dr. Carver,* produced by Pete Smith for the Metro-Goldwyn-Mayer studio and directed by Fred Zinnemann, later to become a top Hollywood filmmaker. An actor played Carver in his younger days, and the scientist portrayed himself as an older man.

The awards and recognition continued to snowball. Several significant honors came in 1939. Carver was awarded an

Ernest Just

It is ironic that while George Washington Carver was becoming a national hero for his relatively insignificant work with peanuts and sweet potatoes, other black scientists were toiling in near obscurity. One of the most significant of these was Ernest Everett Just.

Just (August 14, 1883–October 27, 1941) was a pioneer black U.S. biologist and one of the most respected scientists of his time. Born in Charleston, South Carolina, his parents were determined that he would receive the best education possible. The only black student at the Kimball Union Academy, Just completed the four-year program in just three years and graduated with the highest grades in his class. After graduation, he attended Dartmouth College, earning special honors in botany, history, and sociology, and graduated magna cum laude.

Like all black college graduates of his time, it was impossible for him to find a position teaching at a white college or university, so he took a position at historically black Howard University. In 1910, he was put in charge of the newly formed biology department, and, in 1912, he became head of the Department of Zoology, a position he held until his death in 1941.

Central to his scientific reputation was his research at the Marine Biology Laboratory at Woods Hole, Massachusetts, beginning in 1909, collecting, classifying, and caring for marine specimens. Just published more than 50 scientific papers based on his 20 years at Woods Hole. In addition, he wrote what is considered to be one of the most important textbooks of the twentieth century, *Biology of the Cell Surface* (1939).

Beginning in 1929, feeling certain that racial prejudice was holding him back, Just began performing an extensive amount of research in Europe, which lasted until his return to the United States in 1940, forced by the beginnings of World War II. He died the following year of pancreatic cancer, unknown to the general public.

honorary membership in the American Inventors Society; received a Roosevelt Medal, given in memory of President Theodore Roosevelt; and became the first black person to address a forum sponsored by the *New York Herald-Tribune.*

Despite his revered status, Carver was not immune from the humiliations and absurdities of American racial practices. His lecture tours in the segregated South posed travel and accommodation problems. Jim Crow laws, which called for separate facilities for blacks and whites, prompted friends such as Jimmie Hardwick to drive Carver to speaking engagements so that he would not have to suffer the ignominy of segregation on public transportation. Almost 10 years after Carver was denied a place in a sleeping car on a train trip to Dallas, Texas, because he was black (thereby creating a storm of protest in black newspapers), a visit to New York aroused another controversy. Arriving at the New Yorker Hotel in 1939, Carver and Austin Curtis were told that no rooms were available, although they had reservations. While the 74-year-old Carver waited in a foyer, reporters were called in, and, after more than six hours, the hotel finally assigned the scientist and his assistant to rooms. The hotel management insisted that no racial snub was intended, but the incident caused a flood of editorials in papers throughout the country to decry the treatment Carver had received.

Carver faced this matter while he was in poor health. He had been hospitalized in 1938 with what his doctors diagnosed as pernicious anemia, a serious disease caused by a deficiency of certain stomach and liver secretions; in earlier years, it was usually considered fatal. Carver's doctors began to inject him with a liver extract that contained vitamin B_{12}, a new way to treat the ailment. Although many people, including the scientist himself, feared that he would die, he became well enough by 1939 to return to the laboratory and take on a few speaking engagements. Carver and Austin Curtis continued to work on several projects, but Carver's days as a researcher and creative chemist were largely over. By the late 1930s, under Secretary Henry A. Wallace (the same Henry A. Wallace who as a little boy had taken nature walks with Carver in Ames, Iowa), the USDA was pouring considerable money into agricultural research. The agency set up regional laboratories that were designed to find new uses for surplus crops, and Carver, with his failing health and meagerly funded lab, could hardly match their work.

PRESERVING HIS LEGACY

Carver's last major undertaking was not a research project but an effort to preserve his legacy and to establish a means by which others could carry on his work. During his final years, he turned his attention to setting up the George Washington Carver Museum and Cultural Center and its accompanying foundation in Tuskegee. Curtis proved to be an enormous asset in this effort, drawing up plans and soliciting contributions. In 1938, the institute designated an old laundry building for conversion into a museum and laboratory.

As work on the facility began, Carver, who had lived on campus during his entire career at Tuskegee, moved from a dormitory to a guest house that adjoined the proposed museum so that he could more easily supervise the work in progress. A year later, 2,000 people attended the opening of the partially completed museum. Two years after that, another big crowd flowed into the building for the opening of its art rooms, which displayed Carver's paintings and handicrafts.

Because contributions were modest, the professor himself ended up giving his life savings—$60,000 by the time of his death—to the establishment of the Carver Foundation. In addition to the museum, the foundation set up research fellowships for students to follow in Carver's footsteps. Aware that he was nearing the end of his life, Carver saw the museum and foundation as a way to emphasize and preserve the inspirational qualities of his career.

For similar reasons, Carver also cooperated fully with a writer named Rackham Holt, who was preparing a biography of him for publication by Doubleday, Doran and Company. The elderly scientist agreed to numerous interviews with Holt, and, on reading a draft of her manuscript in 1940, he was delighted with the flattering portrait she had drawn. He called it "the most fascinating piece of writing I have read." Accordingly, Carver became concerned when publication delays arose. In 1942, he wrote to Holt, "I was hoping so much that this book could be finished before it had to close with something sordid. . . ." He was referring to the possibility that he might die before the book's release.

Sadly, the "sordid" thing that Carver feared came to pass before Holt's biography appeared. Late in 1942, Carver made one last trip to Dearborn, Michigan. Henry Ford had just completed building a nutritional lab in Carver's honor and had put up a replica of Carver's childhood home in Ford's outdoor museum, Greenfield Village. The trip must have drained the last of Carver's physical resources, for he was noticeably frail when he returned to Tuskegee in November. Still, he insisted on going about his daily activities until he suffered a painful fall in December while entering the Carver Museum.

Carver died a few weeks later, on the evening of January 5, 1943, at the age of 77. He was buried on the campus of Tuskegee, near the grave of Booker T. Washington.

The flow of honors had continued unabated in the last year of Carver's life: a Thomas A. Edison fellowship, membership in the Laureate Chapter of the Kappa Delta Pi education society, an honorary doctorate from Selma University. There was more to come after his death. His Missouri birthplace was declared a national monument in 1943, an honor that had previously been granted only to Presidents Washington and Lincoln. That same year, a steamship was named after him. A postage stamp in his honor was issued in 1947, and a Polaris submarine was named after him in 1956. He was elected to the Agricultural

1998

© USPS 1998

Though Carver the man had many different sides to his character, as a public figure he became widely celebrated and even mythologized. In 1998, he was honored by the U.S. Postal Service, which printed his image on a first-class stamp.

Hall of Fame in 1969 and to the Hall of Fame for Great Americans in New York in 1973. The two colleges he had attended—Simpson and Iowa State—both dedicated science buildings to him, and Rackham Holt's biography, published in 1943 and revised in 1962, fixed the popular image of Carver—saintly, selfless, brilliant—in the public mind for following generations and served as the standard account of his life and work.

In recent years, historians have demonstrated that Carver was much more complicated than the folk hero who had found such public favor. It is true that he could be kind, generous, and dedicated to serving others. Literally hundreds of people—his students, the young men and women he "adopted" on his lecture tours, and scores of others, both influential and ordinary—were profoundly affected by his personal qualities and admired him deeply. The impact of his personality on countless white Southerners is inestimable. For many, their friendship with Carver opened their eyes to the evil of racial prejudice. As his friend Howard Kester said, "Marvelous are the miracles you have performed in the laboratory but more marvelous still are the miracles you have wrought in the hearts and minds of hundreds of men and women." Carver returned their love and admiration with the same intensity.

Yet, as many of his colleagues at Tuskegee would no doubt have testified, he could also be arrogant, secretive, egocentric, and difficult to work with. Although there were many sides to his character, only the positive ones were publicized when America at large discovered him. Thus, his life became enshrouded in myth.

One unfortunate result of the Carver myth was the extent to which it distorted his scientific accomplishments. Carver lived in an era in which invention and innovation were highly prized, an age in which men like Edison and Ford could become national heroes. To fit the growing legend and the need to create an acceptable black hero, Carver's modest accomplishments in the laboratory were overrated by the press, to such extent that his work with peanuts and sweet potatoes is all that he is generally remembered for. The truly significant features of his work and vision—his praiseworthy efforts to help the poorest of his farmers and his deep love and appreciation of the beauty and unity of nature—were lost in the hoopla.

Relishing the publicity, Carver also seemed to lose sight of his original aims, at least for a time. Late in his life, he admitted to some of his friends that his many years of pursuing the elusive goal of a commercial breakthrough were misguided and self-deceiving. In his drive for acceptance and fame, he had spent too many years away from his significant work searching for a new commercially viable product that would never come.

Nevertheless, Carver remained an inspirational role model for many black Americans, and he has frequently been cited by black organizations and newspapers as one who strove against the odds to be something other than what whites expected blacks to be. There can be no doubt that he opened the hearts and minds of many whites with whom he came in contact, and some of them—such as the social activist Howard Kester—drew inspiration from his example and worked actively against injustice. Also, because Carver was one of the world's best-known black Americans, his well-publicized encounters with racism, such as the sleeping-car incident of 1930 and the New Yorker Hotel incident of 1939, reminded the country of the deficiencies in its system that were yet to be resolved.

Carver's legacy is, to be sure, a mixed one, and when scholars began to reexamine his life and demolish the myths about

IN HIS OWN WORDS...

Dr. Carver felt that these eight cardinal virtues were worthy goals for his students to emulate and strive toward:

1. Be clean both inside and out.

2. Neither look up to the rich or down to the poor.

3. Lose, if need be, without squealing.

4. Win without bragging.

5. Always be considerate of women, children and older people.

6. Be too brave to lie.

7. Be too generous to cheat.

8. Take your share of the world and let others take theirs.

the scientific contributions that surrounded his later career, some suggested that he deserved to be forgotten. Others, taking a more balanced view, emphasized his earlier work at Tuskegee, the impact of his friendships, and the relevance of his particular vision of nature: He always saw the natural world as a unified whole in which each part was related to all the other parts—a view that would find favor among modern-day ecologists and environmentalists.

Out of Carver's love and respect for nature came his emphasis on utilizing resources that were both readily available and easily renewable. In his lifetime, such ideas were steamrollered by the prevailing notion that bigger is better. Indeed, the developers of modern technology have often sent it forward at a headlong pace, pursuing short-term goals at the costly expense of long-term effects. A depleted and polluted environment has been one result of this shortsightedness.

As John Crighton, Carver's colleague and friend, said in his article "Dr. George Washington Carver: Scientist, Humanitarian and Mystic":

> He had the basic philosophy of the environmentalists, the people of the Wilderness Society and the Sierra Club in that he had an appreciation of the mystery and beauty of the universe. . . . The earth to him was not just a treasure-house to be ransacked and to be plundered and to be profited from, but it was of course our home and it's the place of beauty and the mystery. It was God's handiwork, to some extent God's incarnation, you might say. So in these respects, I'm sure that he would today be concerned with problems that did not exist in his time, that is the greenhouse effect and the erosion or destruction of the ozone shield and the ravaging of the rain forests, the pollution of our oceans and inland waterways, of the air that we breathe with smog and so forth. I'm sure that he would be allied with the greater scientists of today in working on these problems which in my opinion will require not

only the scientists to work at but the scientists and the theologians, in other words science and religion—science to find possible solutions and religion to help persuade people to the broad, worldwide view that is necessary for solving them.

Carver was himself partly seduced by the spell cast by the notion that bigger is better, as his failed efforts at commercializing his research demonstrate. He returned to many of his earlier concerns when the Great Depression hit, however, and among his chief aims in establishing the Carver Museum and Foundation was the preservation of his original vision, which he feared was being misunderstood. That became evident when a reporter at the 1941 opening of the museum's art rooms asked him how he had been able to accomplish so many different things.

"Would it surprise you," Carver answered, "if I say that I have not been doing many DIFFERENT things? All these years, I have been doing one thing." He then recited several lines from a poem by Alfred, Lord Tennyson that, in effect, summed up his life:

Little flower—but if I could understand
What you are, root and all, and all in all,
I should know what God and man is

For all of his adult life Carver strove, through his exploration of nature and the world around him, to understand the works of God and man through science and inspiration. His hope, always, was to fulfill what he saw as his mission—to help and to better people. As he said in an interview in late 1917, when asked what motivated him, he replied, "Well, some day I will have to leave this world. And when that day comes, I want to feel that I have an excuse for having lived in it. I want to feel that my life has been of some service to my fellow man."

It is safe to say that Carver's misson, his life goal, was accomplished.

c. 1864 George Washington Carver is born in Diamond, Missouri.

1877 Carver begins his formal education in Neosho, Missouri.

1884 Carver finishes high school in Minneapolis, Kansas.

1885 Highland College in Kansas denies Carver's admission.

1886 Carver becomes a homesteader in Ness County, Kansas.

1890 Carver enrolls at Simpson College in Iowa.

1891 Carver transfers to Iowa State College of Agricultural and Mechanical Arts.

1894 Iowa State awards Carver a bachelor of agriculture degree; he becomes a member of the Iowa State College faculty.

1896 Carver receives a master of agriculture degree; becomes director of agriculture and director of the agricultural experiment station at Tuskegee Institute in Alabama.

1898 Carver begins to issue bulletins on his experiment station work.

1916 Carver is named to the advisory board of the National Agricultural Society; elected a fellow of England's Royal Society for the Encouragement of the Arts.

1918 U.S. Department of Agriculture engages Carver as a consultant in agricultural research.

1919 Carver develops peanut milk.

1921 Carver appears before the House Ways and Means Committee.

1923 Carver awarded the Spingarn Medal; Carver Products Company is formed.

1926 Carver Penol Company is formed.

1928 Simpson College awards Carver an honorary doctor of science degree.

1933   Peanut oil massages widely publicized.

1935   U.S. Department of Agriculture names Carver collaborator to Mycology and Plant Disease Survey.

1938   *The Story of Doctor Carver*, starring Carver, is produced.

1939   George Washington Carver Museum and Foundation at Tuskegee opens to the public.

1943   Carver dies on January 5 in Tuskegee, Alabama.

Further Reading

Ayers, Edward L. *The Promise of the New South: Life After Reconstruction.* New York: Oxford University Press, 1993.

Carroll, Rebecca. *Uncle Tom or New Negro? African Americans Reflect on Booker T. Washington and Up From Slavery 100 Years Later.* New York: Harlem Moon, 2006.

Du Bois, W.E.B. *The Souls of Black Folk.* New York: Penguin, 1966.

Harlan, Louis R. *Booker T. Washington: The Making of a Black Leader, 1856–1901.* New York: Oxford University Press, 1975.

Harlan, Louis R. *Booker T. Washington: The Wizard of Tuskegee, 1901–1915.* New York: Oxford University Press, 1986.

Kremer, Gary R. *George Washington Carver: In His Own Words.* Columbia: University of Missouri Press, 1986.

Moore, Jacqueline. *Booker T. Washington, W.E.B. Du Bois, and the Struggle for Racial Uplift.* Wilmington, Del.: SR Books, 1988.

Ward, Geoffrey C., Ric Burns, and Ken Burns. *The Civil War: An Illustrated History.* New York: Knopf, 1990.

Washington, Booker T. *Up From Slavery.* Lenox, Mass.: Hard Press, 2006.

Williams, Juan, and Julian Bond. *Eyes on the Prize: America's Civil Rights Years, 1954–1965.* New York: Penguin, 1988.

Williamson, Joel. *A Range for Order: Black-White Relations in the American South Since Emancipation.* New York: Oxford University Press, 1986.

Woodward, C. Vann. *Origins of the New South, 1877–1913.* Baton Rouge: Louisiana State University Press, 1971.

WEB SITES

"Black History Month," History.com
www.history.com/minisites/blackhistory

"Encyclopaedia Britannica's Guide to Black History," Encyclopaedia Britannica Online
www.britannica.com/blackhistory

"George Washington Carver," National Park Service
www.nps.gov/gwca

"How to Grow the Peanut and 105 Ways of Preparing it for Human Consumption," Texas A&M University
http://plantanswers.tamu.edu/recipes/peanutrecipes.html

"The Legacy of George Washington Carver," Special Collections Department, Iowa State University Library
www.lib.iastate.edu/spcl/gwc/home.html

Picture Credits

PAGE

3: Library of Congress, ppmsc-03252

5: © Bettmann/CORBIS

6: National Park Service, photo by Charissa Eichman

11: © North WindNorth Wind Picture Archives

15: © Bettmann/CORBIS

23: © North WindNorth Wind Picture Archives

25: Library of Congress, pan-6a04735

29: Prentice Herman Polk, gelatin silver print, gift of P.H. Polk, Collection of California African American Museum

32: Library of Congress, fsa-8302400

36: Library of Congress, ggbain-05046

45: Library of Congress, det-4a13433

50: AP Images

53: AP Images

56: Library of Congress, cph-3d01817

63: Library of Congress, ppmsca-05633

69: © Bettmann/CORBIS

75: © Bettmann/CORBIS

82: AP Images

87: Library of Congress, ggbain-07435

99: AP Images

105: AP Images, Christopher Gannon

COVER

AP Images

Dennis Abrams is the author of several books for Chelsea House, including biographies of Barbara Park, Anthony Horowitz, Hamid Karzai, and the Beastie Boys. He attended Antioch College, where he majored in English and communications. A voracious reader since the age of three, Dennis lives in Houston, Texas, with his partner of 19 years, along with their two dogs and three cats.